THE PEACEFUL WARRIOR

The memoirs of a Damaged Mind and Soul

By

Patrick J. Schnerch

Edited by

Dr. Marc D. Baldwin PhD

Note for Librarians: A cataloguing record for this book is available from Library and Archives
Canada at www.collectionscanada.ca/amicus/index-e.html
ISBN 1-4120-9508-5

Printed in Victoria, BC, Canada. Printed on paper with minimum 30% recycled fibre.
Trafford's print shop runs on "green energy" from solar, wind and other environmentally-friendly power sources.

TRAFFORD
PUBLISHIN

Offices in Canada, USA, Ireland and UK

Book sales for North America and international:
Trafford Publishing, 6E–2333 Government St.,
Victoria, BC V8T 4P4 CANADA
phone 250 383 6864 (toll-free 1 888 232 4444)
fax 250 383 6804; email to orders@trafford.com
Book sales in Europe:
Trafford Publishing (UK) Limited, 9 Park End Street, 2nd Floor
Oxford, UK OX1 1HH UNITED KINGDOM
phone 44 (0)1865 722 113 (local rate 0845 230 9601)
facsimile 44 (0)1865 722 868; info.uk@trafford.com
Order online at:
trafford.com/06-1263

10 9 8 7 6 5 4 3

Acknowledgements

I thank my loving wife Kathy for her love, commitment and understanding.

I want to thank Auntie Jessie and dearly departed Uncle Adam for raising me as one of their own. Special thanks also for allowing me to print her poem on the back cover.

I would like to thank Dr. Marc D. Baldwin PhD for his great job at editing and making this all possible. He believed in my message. Thanks Marc.

I owe a great debt of gratitude to the Groth family for turning me from a delinquent and into a man of honour.

I would like to thank my "Friendly Ghost" for her hard work and dedication making this a quality publication.

I would like to thank Stephan Graham for his guidance throughout the project. He made me realize things that I would never have thought of.

Patrick J. Schnerch

Introduction

It's been one hell of a ride. What you are about to read is a collection of memoirs and journals written by a man living with dual diagnosis. Dual diagnosis is a condition in which mental illness and addiction are the two leading factors to the patient's condition. The ill usually use their drug of choice to numb the effects of their mental anguish. They develop their own self medicate program. However, this only contradicts the medication and treatment the doctor has prescribed.

I believe that these writings could be beneficial to others who may have similar experiences. Millions of people are affected by these conditions worldwide.

Living a life that should have never been is the best description of a tortured mind. Hereditary...maybe it was. Trauma...that is also possible. Life became unbearable and my mind shut off, blocking horrible memories from destroying me. The darkness became my sanctuary. This was my world away from reality.

Deep in the folds of darkness, I would hide from anything that could hurt me. This happened fairly early in childhood. Alone, I would weep for death to come and take me. For over thirty years, death was very welcome in my heart. Even today, the wish has not gone away. Sorrow is all I know.

After decades of torment, pride and self-esteem are nonexistent. Personal-hygiene is not a factor, nor is clean clothes or caring what people think. Being unemployed is the worst feeling in the world. Self-worth has no meaning in my vocabulary.

Finally, I found something that would make it all go away, at least temporarily. Alcohol became the magic elixir. I would rot at the bottom of a whiskey bottle for years, sending me deeper into the abyss. Medications do not have the desired affect, but booze does. It numbs the mind and makes all the pain go away. This was my freedom away from the relentless torture, freedom from the hurt and agony. The darkness then consumed me whole, not leaving any resemblance of what I used to be.

I used to be a man. However, the name does not apply anymore. An empty shell is more like it. I pay room and board to my wife of twenty-three years. We pass each other in silence like two ships in the night. There is no relationship other than the marriage certificate stating that there is one. Friends and family have been abandoned so that the solitude is not disturbed. As you can see, I am already dead. It's just that my body doesn't know it yet. There is no will to continue any further; all is lost.

It has been a tough battle fighting the yearning for death. Peace and tranquility is all I seek. The overwhelming power of the entity has been postponed for three decades. Now, I am getting too tired to fight.

Is this how it will all end, or is there something I can do? An idea has come to mind. A careful examination of my past will reveal where the pain came from. Excavating my life will be a painful journey, and I want to share it with you. We'll start from the very beginning and unearth the roots. Maggots consume my soul, there has to be something rotting deep inside of me. Perhaps by reliving the past and digging up painful memories, I might be able to accept the past and put it all behind me.

This is a desperate attempt to resolve my troubles and perhaps start a new life free from the darkness that has engulfed me for so long. As for now, I don't have any emotions or feelings anymore. I don't hear the birds sing in the morning or feel the warmth of a sunny day. There is no color in my life, just shades of black. Something has to happen, and it lies deep within my soul where the secrets are hidden even from me.

It is time to emerge from the darkness or die trying. Traveling those old roads again will be very moving and somewhat painful. This is the only way to break free from its grip on me. Coming full circle to see myself in the mirror and face these demons will be horrific at times. These shadows have overseen most of my life; it is time to set myself free.

The Early Years

My memory starts off with my growing up with a loving mother who smothered me with hugs and kisses. It was a wonderful relationship. My father was stern in appearance. Deep inside that rough exterior was a kind man but I was apprehensive of him for I could not predict his mood, especially when he was drinking. He adored my mother, but the alcohol buried this kind heart. They had two older children, one was Dave and the older sister was Eleanor. They both moved out very shortly after my arrival and memory. I have very little recollection of them when I was growing up as a toddler.

It was the early nineteen-sixties in a rural area of Camp Morton, Manitoba where I began my life. This location is situated seventy miles South of Winnipeg.

Growing up on a hobby farm was a secure and safe environment. Swamp and trees, mainly poplar and spruce, surrounded the farm. The white birch trees gave depth to the bush. A few hundred feet to the North West was the old barn. The red paint was peeling and revealed the old weathered grey wood. The shingles on the roof were in bad repair; many were missing, which left a patchwork pattern. Outside the barn was the water trough and well for the cows. For the longest time, a hand pump drew the water. Watering the cows became my chore. The trough was an old oil barrel split in half and welded end to end.

A half a mile away was a gravel pit where the big gravel trucks would go and transport gravel and sand to various excavation sites in the area. That's why we had so much dust. We were on their main routes. Clouds of yellow dust would float over the house causing a thick layer on the windows. You would literally choke if you were outside at the time that they passed the property. Our driveway was about two hundred feet long of gravel and dirt. It led from the road that the big gravel trucks used to speed on causing dust to cover all of Mom's freshly cleaned laundry. The dust was so bad that the vegetable leaves had a layer of yellow dust on them.

To the west of the barn were two grey weathered log sheds with wooden shingles. One building was the grain shed. I never liked going in there because I hated mice and rats. They were always in there. Thank goodness for Bullet. That was our barn cat. She would have kittens every spring. When my Dad milked the cows, I would go with him and feed the cats. Then Bullet would take her family to hunt in the grain shed and keep the rodent population down.

When Bullet had kittens, I could hear little meows coming from the loft. She would keep her kittens warm by burrowing deep between the stored hay bales. I would follow the meows and lift the bales to reveal a record number, each time, of cute little kittens. I would welcome each one of them into this world with hugs and kisses. Then I would count them and put them back and return the bales of hay to their original place so the kittens could stay warm. After returning them to their little home, I would run to the house and report to my Mom the discovery. I was all smiles that we had cute kittens.

The other building in front of the grain shed was the piggy barn and fenced pen. I had to feed the pigs. They became very stupid and aggressive when it came time to feed them their slop of milk and vegetable peelings. They would put their feet in the food trough fighting for their position to eat first. There was pushing and shoving, snorting, grunting, and squealing with joy. They were truly pigs in every sense of the word.

I had other chores such as collecting chicken eggs. The chicken coop was to the west of the yard past the tall yard light. It was a grey log building with weathered grey shingles. Grandpa built it a whole two generations back. I used to hate collecting eggs because these little birds called barn swallows also shared the coop with the chickens staying out of the weather. Once I stood at the entrance, I would startle the barn swallows, and they would swish around inside at what seemed to be a hundred miles an hour in a panic. Then they would gather their thoughts and make their escape by swooping over my head and out the door to safety. Those things used to scare me because they would only fly only inches over my head, which forced me to duck down.

The chickens were not terribly friendly either; they were, at times, quite aggressive and noisy. No matter what would happen, I would still gather eggs for my mother every morning. I also had to feed the chickens grain. I would just dump a can of it in the yard, and they would come squawking from all directions. They ran free in the yard and ate little stones and pebbles to help their digestion of the food.

In front of the chicken coop, there were two huge gas tanks hoisted on wooden stands. Dad would have the gas man come and fill the tanks with fuel so that Dad didn't have to buy gas anywhere else. He fuelled up at home. One tank was regular gas while the other was purple gas used for the farm vehicles, including the truck. The purple gas was cheaper than the regular and only farmers were allowed to use it.

We had a little grey log tool shed to the southeast of the chicken coop. I used to like tinkering around with Dad's tools and gadgets. I spent a lot of time going through his stuff. We had one more tool shed to the southeast of the house where Dad parked the tractor and where his tools and spare tires were kept.

South West was the calves' yard and shed. We would separate the calves from the adult cows so that they wouldn't be harassed. There they would graze and live a life of luxury until they became old enough to join the others. If they were female, they would count their blessings because they became milking cows. If they were male, in a couple of years they would become steak.

To the east was the huge vegetable garden, which was about three hundred yards long by twenty-five yards wide. We also had another large garden beside it for corn, potatoes, and raspberries. This kept us well fed for the winter. Mom worked in the garden every day during the summer. She had tons of work to do.

When I was only a toddler in the wintertime, my Mom had to go and feed the cows hay. She would not leave me in the house by myself so she would bundle me up in my parka, wool hat, mittens and scarf and trudge four hundred feet to the east in knee-deep snow. There the cows would come from the barnyard to eat their lunch. Mom would break open and split two bales of hay for them. I would stand off in a distance and watch my breath hit the cold winter air. My little cheeks would get really rosy.

In the summer time, my Mom would harvest the garden and freeze vegetables for the wintertime. Of course, there was a lot of peelings and waste. This really wasn't waste at all. My Mom would give me the pails to dump over the cows' fence and give them a treat. The cows loved potatoes peelings, cornhusks, and old lettuce leaves. They'd eat it all up and never leave anything.

I also had to feed milk to the calves. They were stupid animals. They got so frantic at feeding time that they would run across the yard and almost put their head through the bottom of the pail. I held the pail with one hand cradling the bottom and one hand holding the handle. The calves got so frantic that they would get the handle caught over their heads, which would pinch my fingers. That really hurt, and I used to get so mad at them. Finally, I got smart and kept a big stick by the fence. Every time they got stupid, I would crack them between the eyes and knock some sense into them.

My true love and constant companion was my dog. He followed me everywhere and licked my face when he was happy. Since we were so isolated with no friends and I was the only child there, my dog became my best friend. All our pets lived outdoors. The dog would go into the chicken coop and lie on the yellow, musty straw to stay warm from the cold, and the cats would stay in the barn. No animals were allowed in the house. My dog got so excited when I came outside to play with him. In the wintertime, I used to tease him with the sled rope so that he could pull me across the yard. Our ditch outside the front of the property had deep snow banks where I would make toboggan paths to slide down. In between construction, I would throw snowballs at the dog and play with him. He was always by my side. I would play all day in the ditch.

If it were too miserable outside, I would play in the basement. I had all the toys I ever needed to make a farm with my toy metal barn, tractors, combines, and animals. My farm scenes were very elaborate, and they spread across the floor many times blocking the path my mom used to get to the freezer. My dad had to be careful as well to walk around so he could put wood in the furnace in the morning.

I would use the cracks in the cement as roads for my farm trucks. I used to play all day down there. My imagination would run wild with enthusiasm. I would copy the layout that our farm had, including fences and trees and even a dog. Even though I was mainly alone, I was very happy and content.

Our house was huge and took a lot of wood to warm up the concrete walls. Some how, Dad managed to keep the house nice and cozy. I think the wood stove Mom used to cook on used to help keep the kitchen and living room nice and warm. Dad cut wood all summer long to make sure we were warm over the winter. My brother Dave would come home and help Dad cut the trees and brings them home to cut and chop into useable logs for the furnace. One time - they noticed something in the branches as the tree fell. To their amazement, it was a baby owl. He was scared and kept getting his claw hooked into his wing. So they brought it home so the family could see this magnificent creature. I was in awe. The owl was well behaved sitting quietly on the kitchen floor. My dad would try to fix his wing, but the bird quickly got it hooked up again. After making sure that the owl was all right, my dad took it back into the bush to be with its mother.

We had rows and rows of wood piled at the east end of the farm. We would bring the wood to the house and throw it through the basement window, and it was my job to stack it by the furnace to dry out.

The house had five bedrooms; I actually slept in what would have been an extremely large living room. This was also used to store the piano and give me room to play indoors. Upstairs were two bedrooms. One was used by my brother for privacy since he was much older than I. Off from my bedroom were Mom and Dad's bedroom and the spare room where Dave would make out with his girlfriend who later became his loving wife.

The living room was a room intended to be a large dining room. Here we would each find our favourite chair and have our dinner and watch Ed Sullivan on the black and white TV. We didn't have use for a dining room. I did eat my breakfast at the kitchen table. Dad used to have his porridge and coffee in the kitchen, hours before I got up. Dad had many chores to do before he had to go to work.

For a while, we had a hand pump at the kitchen sink to draw the water. We did not have a toilet with running water. In the basement we had a little partition and a pail, which we used when it was cold out. Other than that, we had an outhouse four hundred feet to the northwest of the main house. Mom painted the shingled exterior a hot pink. It was gaudy. It had a green asphalt sheet for a roof. In the wintertime at night, we had a pail in the corner of the kitchen sitting on top of spread out newspapers. This is where I would go instead of trucking across the yard in my long underwear and parka. In the summer time, my mom used to get mad at the men because they were too lazy to walk across the yard to the outhouse for a pee. We would stand off the stoop where Mom would hang her clothes out to dry. There we would pee, and the summer sun would cook the ammonia and cause a big stench.

She hated us for that. I'm sure she would've done the same thing if she weren't built differently.

Under the stoop, that is where the dog dug a deep hole in the shade to lie down in. He would sleep there away from the blistering hot summer sun. Mom tried filling the hole a few times, but soon gave up because the dog would immediately dig it out again. Then she figured that it was only one hole and it is out of the way from things, so she let him stay there in his cool spot.

For those who don't know what a stoop is, it is like a mini patio with support beams underneath to support a laundry stand. It is big enough to stand on and place the laundry tub on the floor to gain access to the clothesline. Ours was to the right of the front door adjacent to the concrete stairs.

As for bathing, this was a bit of a chore since we didn't have running water. Daily, we would take a basin of heated water from the stove and sponge bath. On the weekend, Dad would bring up the galvanized bathtub from the basement and put it by the heating vent in my large bedroom. Taking turns, we would all have a bath. Mom heated pails and pails of water on the wood stove.

Our kitchen had old plywood yellow cupboards and a green and grey square tile pattern on the floor. The wood stove was in the corner by the kitchen table. I remember the smell of the smoke from the stove; it was especially nice when Mom baked bread in it. The loaves came out with a beautiful golden brown crunchy crust and a soft and chewy inside. It was delicious with homemade butter made from the cream from our own cows. Mom had a glass butter churn in which she would attach Dad's electric drill to churn the cream. We were modernized.

In the southeast corner of the basement was the potato bin. Here my Mom stored the potatoes and onions for the winter. She'd put the vegetables in the darkest, coldest corner of the house and cover them with soil. There they would stay fresh all winter long. The potatoes would even continue growing roots while in the bin. It did smell quite musty though, but it worked. Mom stored her pickles and relishes down in the basement as well.

When Dad milked the cows, he would then bring the milk to the house and pour it into the electric cream separator. This machine would separate the heavy cream from the milk. My mom and dad would then collect the cream from the week and put it into a cream can and leave the can at the side of the road. The cream truck would come by and pick up the cream and take it to the plant. Once a month, Mom and Dad would receive a cheque for the cream. We also kept some for raspberry dessert. My Mom would also make my Dad's favourite salad of shredded lettuce, cream, and green onion. He ate that everyday with a large piece of homemade bread and butter. Mom used to also use the cream to make Ukrainian-style homemade Borsht. That is a creamed red beet soup. It was a favourite in our family.

I used to like to help Dad with the cows at milking time. I would open the door and let the cows in and chain them in their stalls. Then I would feed them chop, which was a feed consisting of wheat chopped into a powdered feed. Each cow got some hay to keep them busy while Dad milked them. My dad had a sense of humour because the cats would wait patiently for their dinner of warm fresh milk. As Dad was milking, he would spray the cats with fresh milk directly from the cow. It was the cutest thing to see them try to catch the milk in their mouths. Usually, they got pretty wet and would spend the rest of the night licking them clean.

Our roof was wooden grey shingles with heavy moss on the - north side. The roof was original and was never replaced. It did need repair, but it was never done. The outside was lime green stucco with yellow patches, complete with numerous cracks. Although old, this was home sweet home. We had a beautiful veranda, or deck as we call it today, at the front of the house facing the yellow gravel road. The floor was rotten, but I just stepped over the holes and broken boards.

When my Dad worked for the fishing plant, he used to bring home lots of fish. He would clean them up, and the cats would gather around him for their tidbits. They loved fish guts and heads. My Dad was a great provider. We always had lots of food to eat. Most of the food was taken right from the farm itself. The only things we bought from the store were sugar, tobacco, and flour. I always got twenty-five cents for a bag of chips and a soda.

I remember in the spring, my Dad would kill and clean chickens for the freezer. I never liked it when he did that, so I used to keep a good distance away. The panic of the chickens made me feel sorry for them. Even though I didn't like them, it was sad to see them die.

Wintertime would approach, and the freezer meat was almost depleted. It was time to butcher a steer or a pig. Friends, neighbours, and aunts and uncles would arrive to help out. I was never allowed to watch the actual killing of the animal. I was always kept in doors away from this shocking, but necessary action.

The men would shoot the animal and kill it. Then with a tractor and lift, which was, a device used to secure a bucket for digging, but with the bucket removed it then became a hoist. There were two iron beams to which they attached the animal's rear legs to string him up in the air. They would then transport the carcass to the butchering area. There they would cut the throat and collect the blood for Kieshka, which is more commonly known as blood pudding. It is a black sausage made of blood and buckwheat, very good stuff.

The women would boil water so that the men could wash the meat clean of blood. I had an uncle who was a butcher by trade, and he did everyone's butchering. He would torch the hide to melt the fat and pull the hide away from the carcass. This would leave black smoke marks on the meat, which had to be washed down. They would remove the hide being careful not to contaminate the meat.

Once the hide was removed and the carcass washed clean, they would then cut the animal and remove parts such as heart and liver for eating. They would then discard the guts onto a wooden sled to be later dumped in the bush for the wildlife. After the cavity is washed out with water, the carcass is then split in half.

Then after a final washing, the meat would be taken down and put into the cool basement to hang up from the joists so that the meat can properly age. That is what was involved with butchering while I was growing up on the farm.

When I was six years old, I was watching the TV in the living room one morning when my mom received a phone call. She seemed excited. When she hung up the phone she told me that Dad was now a grandpa. Without saying a word and saddened with grief, I stood on the couch and stared out into the driveway.

I stood there from early morning till dad came home. My mother had no idea what was going through my head. I didn't eat my lunch or go outside to play that day. I was thinking of how my grandpa looked with his wrinkled skin, white hair, and his slow shuffle when he walked. I expected that now that Dad was a grandpa, he is going to come home looking like that too. I was very depressed. I didn't want my dad to change.

Four o'clock arrived, and I still hadn't moved from my perch at the window. Then the dog barked, and Dad drove into the driveway. I gulped with panic and fear. Soon the moment of truth would be here. My dad got out of the truck like any other day and walked to the porch. To my extreme amazement, he hadn't changed at all. I jumped off the couch like a rabbit and yelled with excitement, "He's the same!!" My mom turned around dumbfounded at my sudden burst of energy. I ran through the kitchen and jumped onto my dad's leg. With tears in my eyes, I mumbled, "Dad, you're the same."

Growing Pains

My brother and dad sometimes had to make chop for the cows. This was an extremely dusty and dirty job. They would put on their coveralls and hook up a belt from the tractor flywheel to the flywheel of the grain chopper. They would put a half twist into the belt and back the tractor up until the belt was tight. Once the chopper was operational, they would shovel wheat into the hopper. The chopped grain would come out of a chute in the bottom and into the chop bin. When finished, they had this white powder all over their bodies, in their hair, and on their eyebrows. I never had to make chop, but I watched them carefully.

Another big job was cutting the trees into small enough logs for the furnace. This was also done with the tractor and belt. The belt would be attached to the flywheel pulley of a three-foot saw blade. The tree would be put into an iron cradle. The cradle would then be pushed forward, thus cutting the tree into useable logs. The logs would then be put onto a pile to be later split into smaller pieces and stacked.

My mom and dad were very hard workers. They provided a home and plenty of food for the family. Mixed with love, it was a cozy setting to grow up in. I will never forget what they did for me; I am forever grateful.

I did have cousins come over to play me with sometimes. As I got older, I was allowed to ride my bike to their places to play. Times were spent in the gravel pit, summer for swimming, and winter for tobogganing and skating. There was the mother load of raspberry bushes behind a particular hill that only my cousin Michael and I knew about. This was found by accident as we played "King of the Castle" on top of the hill. He threw me into the thorns. To my surprise, there were millions of red, ripe raspberries. I never saw so many in my life.

Michael and I used take the 22 cal. rifle and go target shooting in the pit or snowmobiling in the wintertime. Michael's dad always had a lot of chores for Michael to do. Many times, if I wanted to spend time with Michael, I had to work too, either picking up hay or numerous other jobs. The one thing about working for my Uncle Ignus was that Aunty Annie fed me extremely well. I was never hungry when I was there. They always treated me like one of the family. Auntie Annie is my dad's sister; she has the same kind heart as he does.

I love that family. They were extremely good to me. In the summer time, they would take me to Paulin's Picnic. Paulin's was a candy manufacturer situated in Winnipeg. One of my older cousins worked there, and I was allowed to join the family in the festivities. There were games, hot dogs, hamburgers, and all the fixings of a fun-filled day. There was the three-legged race and the potato sack race - I never won, but I always had fun. These were fond memories of my Uncle Ignus and Auntie Annie. Uncle Ignus has recently passed on leaving behind his wife and nine kids with numerous grandchildren. God bless his soul.

There was one thing that could have caused troubles, and that was living with an alcoholic father whom many years passed before I understood that he was my Uncle Adam and not my biological father. I was very distant from him during those formative years. I was actually scared of him for I never knew how he would react. It wasn't until many years later that we built a loving relationship. Only well after he quit drinking did I ever see the gentleness of this man.

During those early years, he was quite verbally abusive and mean-spirited towards my mother. This used to hurt me deeply for I didn't like when my mom was hurting inside. He would be quite angry at the world when he drank and was not approachable. He did not show affection during those years. He was quite rough in his demeanour.

When my mom cried, so did I. She later explained to me that it was very difficult living with him while he was drinking during that time. I rarely showed him any affection because of my fears. I had seen him on many occasions being quite aggressive and angry. It took decades before I let my guard down around him. I was very apprehensive about his presence. Not only did I respect him, I was also afraid of him.

This could have been the contributing factor to my trouble dealing with the men, even now. I have very little trust for my fellow man and am usually apprehensive when confronted by their appearance. I find more comfort when dealing with a woman than I do a man. I find them less threatening to my nature, which puts me more at ease. I have a difficult time bonding with men for I do not share in their beliefs and rituals of becoming a man. I followed Jesus and the path that he made for me. A quiet and sombre existence is the way I choose to live my life. This meek and mild manner of living is more suitable to my likings.

We had our rough times, for Dad was a heavy drinker. He didn't drink every day, but when he did, he always got pissed. This was when the nasty part of him would come out. Since we lived in a rural area, the police presence on the roads was nonexistent. There were many nights when, driving home from a drunk, he would slide the truck into the ditch in the middle of winter. It was a blessing that we were not killed for this was a common practice for many years. It was a difficult time living with Dad like that.

When we went out to either a cousin or uncle's place in the evening, I knew that we would be there for a long haul. The bottles came out and the children were then brushed off to play somewhere out of sight. At this time, the children did not exist. Their wills and wants were seldom met while the adults were drinking. This would continue till late at night. I remember falling asleep while hanging onto Mom's knee. She would try to persuade Dad to drink up and go home, but Dad always poured another one just to spite her. All the other kids that lived there already had their pyjamas on and were in bed hours before.

Our lives were consumed by alcohol. It ran our lives--especially mine. I no longer had a father; all my insecurities fell onto my mother. Being extremely mild mannered myself, I found those activities very disturbing. Perhaps, during these formative years, was my very own undoing. Even though there was no physical abuse, I was still scared to death.

I couldn't get close to him. We never touched hearts. I tried to show my affection only to be turned away. He was able to shun his family away, especially when drinking. His stare was dramatically frightening.

This could have been the very first time that I would hide in the folds of darkness away from the realities that could hurt me. There, I would block out the hurt of having an alcoholic father. This is when my heart and soul died. It is here that I hid away from the truths for over four decades. I couldn't handle the truth, so I made them go away. The darkness became my sanctuary. This is where I had a quiet peace of mind away from the hurt. My mild manners did not allow me to fight back. I became a victim to the darkness in order to remain sane.

Alcohol was a family staple. Most of my uncles were also heavy drinkers. My dad would feed off of them and stay out until late at night with them. As heavy as he drank, he never missed a day of work in his life. He never complained that he was too ill to function the next day; all the work and chores were done on time. My dad never made an excuse. He knew he had a problem, and he never let it rule his life. He still worked and ran a farm at the same time.

He would get up at four in the morning and take care of the cows, eat breakfast, and go to work. After that, there was the milking and feeding of the cows and in the summer time he would go to the fields and work till late at night. I never saw him for months because he was working during all my waking hours. My mother told me that my dad came home late one night from the fields and was standing over me while I was sleeping with a tear in his eye. My mom asked, "What's wrong?"

My dad replied, "I never see Pat anymore. He's growing so big, and I'm not around to see it."

My mom was sympathetic and saw the gentleness of this man. This is the man she married, not the alcoholic.

Some of my fondest moments were the times I had with our dog. This was the first dog I remember and he was a black border collie. During the warm summer months, Mom would make me a sandwich and a glass of fruit drink for lunch. She would also make up a big slice of bread layered thick with lard so that the dog could have lunch with me on the veranda.

The days were sunny and warm and we would sit in the shade of the veranda. We could smell the sweet aroma of the lilac trees blowing gently across the deck. My dog would be so excited to get his lunch that he would pounce all over me until I gave it to him.

There was one day that we were about to have a lunch, but I forgot his bread on the kitchen counter. I put my lunch down and ran into the house to get his treat. When I came back, I was astonished, angry, and deeply hurt that he ate my lunch while I was away. I felt betrayed by my best friend. How could he do such a thing? I was so hurt that I cried all afternoon. I didn't even tell Mom what happened. She would have simply made me another one, but my trust was broken. After that I would chase him away when he followed. The bond was broken; it took several days to make retribution with him again.

There was one time when I did him wrong. I don't remember why I decided to hit him with my skipping rope, but I did. I watched him growl and get angry, yet I still continued. Finally he had enough of that shit and attacked me. He viscously bit my head and arms. My mom had to come out of the house and used a broom to get him off of me. I learned my lesson to be kind to animals from that point forward.

Numerous stitches later and no hard feelings, we continued our friendship like two peas in a pod. You would never find one without the other.

We would spend the whole day in the bush seeking new adventures. We would make forts and tree houses, which only consisted of one or two boards, but we did it. We had chores, too. In the afternoon, it was our job to find the cows and chase them home for milking. With no one else to play with, secluded away from neighbours, my dog was my true friend. My dogs were always were special to me since my cousins were much older than I was and near the time for when they were moving out to start their own lives. My dogs were my only companions I had for my first five years of life. There was no one else to play with, so my heart always melted with theirs. I would talk to them and tell them my troubles and they always listened. I never felt alone for as long as we had a dog. I loved them dearly.

My dog had a habit of sitting on the dirt driveway watching the cars go by. One very terrible day, a car hit him. My dog yelped and cried and dragged himself across two large yards and went under the hayrack. There he lay in agony. It was some time later that the shock would set into my little body. I saw a man with a rifle among a group of other men and my dad surrounding my dog. I had a large lump in my throat; I could not help but think that there will never be another beautiful day again without him. Momentarily, I heard a single shot that could be heard around the world ending my friendship and love I had in my heart. Suddenly, it was over. I wasn't quite five years old when I died a second time.

One day after that incident, my mother was making my bed when she heard talking. My window leads to the veranda where my dog and I had our lunch. There I was with my sandwich and fruit drink with a piece of thick bread with lard. There were no signs of an attempt to have lunch even though hours have passed.

She heard me say, *"Why did you have to die? I miss you so much. It's not fun anymore without you. We used to play and run around together, and now you're not here. I made a sandwich for you. It's your favourite; please come back."*

Even though it is almost four decades since then, my mother still remembers that time when I melted her heart.

My mother has just recently told me that my father checked out the car tracks after the incident and saw that they swerved intentionally onto the driveway. It wasn't an accident. He did it on purpose. One of the neighbours chased him and caught up with him. I don't know what happened after that.

He took away my heart the day he murdered my friend. I can't believe that an adult would do that to a little boy. That was the most gut wrenching experience I had to go through at that time. Today, I pray for my dog's soul and remember all the good times we had together. Good dog!

Every wedding anniversary, Dad would take Mom and me for a ride after dinner. He would then stop the truck on the ridge and walk into the bush. Some time would pass, and Dad would come back with a huge bouquet of beautiful wild flowers for Mom. He did this every year for over five decades.

He had a tough exterior, and as a little boy I was somewhat apprehensive of approaching him. Later he changed jobs from the fishing plant to be a sanitation technician or garbage man. I remember those very formative years where my dad would bring home toys, trucks, and bicycles for me. Some were in good shape, and some needed fixing. My dad would give me a truck with the wheels missing and tell me to fix it. I did that and took the finished product to my dad for his approval. I relished every word that came out of his mouth. They were words of wisdom, experience, and knowledge. I was proud to make him happy when that truck was operational and useful again.

After a while, instead of toys, he then was bringing home radios to fix. I would repair and then give it back to dad to use in the garage. As a little boy, I remember my dad coming home in the evening. I could hear the roar of the big truck coming down the roads from miles away. Our new dog was also a beautiful, longhaired border collie that would go to the edge of the driveway every night and wait for Dad to come home. The dog knew well before we did that Dad was on his way home.

Both the dog and I anticipated the arrival of Dad. I don't know which one of us was more excited than the other. The truck would drive in, and the dog would run circles around the truck with a big waggy tail. I would patiently wait for my dad to get out of the truck, give him a big, "Hi Dad!" He would hand me his thermos and lunch box to carry to the porch for him. Then I would open it up and eat the last, dry and curled bologna sandwich as a treat before dinner. What I didn't know is that Mom would make a special sandwich just for me when Dad came home. It wasn't that he was too full to eat it, but it was an extra one. I used to get great joy seeing him come home. He always brought me something to play with that he found. These were truly happy times.

There is a faint memory of my brother (Actually, cousin and Uncle Adam's real son.) living at home and, I believe, my sister Eleanor (Uncle Adam's older child.), who is the oldest, had already left the house. I know this for I remember her trying on her wedding dress when I was very young. My brother was around for a while because I remember him borrowing the truck to go to play hockey or play in his band. There is a great difference in age between us. There was a time that Dave entered a talent show in the city and the family got to watch him on the black and white TV. We were so proud of him and his band; they were really good.

Christmas was truly the happiest day of the year. A couple of weeks prior to Christmas, Dad would take the chainsaw and go into the bush to bring home a Christmas tree. He would put the tree in the stand so it stood up straight. Mom and I would then decorate the tree. We spent the afternoon fixing up the tree and drinking hot chocolate. This was a lot of fun, but the big day was still to come.

With much anticipation and patience, Christmas day arrived. By the afternoon, we were washing up and dressing into our Sunday clothes. We were going to Grandma and Grandpa's house for dinner. They had twelve children. Now they are all grown up with kids of their own. Some of my aunts and uncles also had large families. So there was a large crowd of at least ninety people for dinner.

All my aunts would help out Grandma by bringing over turkeys, hams, desserts, and everything else you could imagine. There were always lots of kids for me to play with. Grandpa made sure there was a lot of booze in the house, for this day was also a special time to get pissed with your family.

Upon arrival at Grandma's house, I would see one of my uncles with the horse rigged to the stone boat, (wooden sled). On top of that were bales of hay and hordes of cousins going for a ride. I would run like mad to the horse and give him a big Christmas hug and climb on the stone boat. This was true adrenalin pumping through my veins. I was made to have fun.

The kids played outside well into the dark when we would then play hide-and-seek. Hours would pass by like minutes as my aunts were getting dinner ready for the tables. Of course, my uncles were already hammered and not caring if they ate or not. Grandma had sawhorses with plywood on top in the basement covered in white bed sheets to make up tables. They made great tables, and they were all covered with tons of delicious food. I remember always really enjoying eating. It's a passion of mine still.

Finally after all that time, the children were called in to get ready for dinner. We all worked up a big appetite playing outside in the snow. You could smell the turkeys filling the house with an enticing aroma. We would get our winter clothes off, and the families would find their place to sit.

Grandpa had two Christmas trees. He had one in the living room and one in the basement. That was really neat; I never knew anyone else having two of them. We found our seats and sat down as a family. I was snuggled between my mom and dad. There was food from one end of the table to the next. It was amazing!!

We would all say our prayers and give thanks for this gift of food and family. We sure had a lot to be thankful for. Then it was time to eat. Mom would serve and cut up my food for me, and I would shovel this stuff down as fast as it was coming. Nothing slowed me down. The food was so good that it felt like I had died and gone to Heaven. This was the one day out of the year that I would really pig out and enjoys myself. It didn't matter how sick I felt later. I would still pack it in.

After eating like a pig, I would burp and fart like the rest of the family. It felt like a gale storm with that sudden rush of warm air. Everyone would loosen their belts and take a sigh of relief. My dad also loved his food. He worked hard, and he ate hard. His mouth was like dangerous machinery when he was eating. You had to be careful that your limbs didn't get in the way.

All had a good time. The women would clear the tables, and the men would stack the sawhorses and plywood in the corner of the basement. The kids now had a place to play indoors. However, play was not on our minds. Very soon, Santa Clause was coming to the house with presents! We would get all so anxious waiting for his arrival.

The children would all gather in the front porch waiting for Santa Clause. You could usually hear his bells ring and his mighty laugh. He would stomp on the steps so very loudly that all the children can hear him. We rustled for our place in line to see who got their present first. Soon, the man in the red suit would arrive.

My aunts were just finishing putting the food away and washing the dishes. My uncles were yet finishing off another bottle of whiskey. Unknowingly to the children, this was Santa's clue to make his entrance.

With much excitement, we heard the ringing of his bells and jolly laugh as he stomped up the stairs. The children would yell, "Santa's here!" The door opened and the children would swarm around him like bees to a hive. Stumbling and tripping over the children, he finally found his chair in the kitchen. I was usually near the end of the line getting all nervous because I was going to see Santa Claus.

Patiently, I would wait my turn. Finally, after an eternity, I would hop on his lap and carefully examine his face. He had blue eyes, rosy cheeks, red nose, a silver beard, and a stench of whiskey on his breath. I would tell him that I was a good boy, and I would ask Mom to confirm my statement. After a short talk, I would get my gift and race into the living room to rip the paper off. It was usually a brand new toy from Santa's workshop up North.

Everyone was having a great time, then it was off to church for midnight Mass. All my aunts and uncles and cousins would pack up and swerve down over the white line to church. It was mainly just our family who packed the place to the rafters. After our prayers and blessings, we would go home to bed and dream sweet thoughts of a wonderful day. This was one of my fondest memories growing up.

Patrick J. Schnerch

Lightning strikes twice

I had aunt and uncle who used to come over on a regular basis to play cards and drink. They would get so involved with themselves that they would never check on the children. My aunt and uncle had an older son and two daughters. The youngest daughter was much older than I was, but she still liked playing games with me. Her brother, who was almost an adult, he used to sit in with the adults or watch TV.

I was not even five years old, but I still remember a game that I didn't like. It didn't matter whose house it was; my cousin would find a secluded room away from the adults and take me with her. She was always wearing a dress. That seemed quite normal at that time. She would lie on the bed with her feet on the floor and open her legs. She then took my hand and guided it under her dress.

I never saw what was under her dress, but I know that my fingers were wet and stinky and that I didn't like that game. She gently coaxed me to continue. When I drew back, she would use a trade-off.

I used to like the smoothness of lady's legs and especially nylons because they were silky soft. I would rub my check on my sister's leg and turn to putty. She thought it was weird, but kinda cute. My cousin would use this weakness to trade pleasures. It always seemed that when I was rubbing my cheek, her brother would come in and say that I had smelled her feet. That wasn't true; I just liked the silk. Four years old, I was easily coached.

This happened on several occasions and was never related to anyone else. It has stayed a secret for forty years. Not until last year did I ever reveal the details of those incidents. I was having sexual abuse therapy and this was one of the deep secrets that came to the forefront. I have never contacted the abuser about this; she probably believes that I was too young to remember.

Apparently, this abuse did not cause any adverse effects that required further treatment. It seemed that I was able to cope with this with no ill effects. Perhaps, one day I will confront her and let her know that I do remember and that her secret is not safe.

Around the same time and involving the same people, I did something that would destroy the kinship between two brothers for the rest of their lives.

I used to see my dad periodically pull a blue box from the top shelf of his closet. I became curious as to what it was. Days later, when I was alone in the house, I got a chair and opened the cupboard to see what was so interesting. To my surprise, it was money!! Lots of it, too!! What I didn't know was that my dad did not have a bank account. This was his life savings. I quickly put it back where it was and put the chair back.

I never saw so much money in my life! I was amazed. Then one day, my aunt and uncle came over for one of their regular visits. My cousin also came over. While the adults were playing cards and drinking, I grabbed my cousin and told her I had a secret. I asked her to promise not to tell anyone. I then took her to Dad's bedroom, got the chair, and opened the cupboard. Then I brought down the blue box for her to see. She was shocked, but I made her promise that it was our secret. I then put everything back the way it was and that was about it.

The following week, that same aunt came over to play cards and drink. My dad asked my uncle for repayment of a loan of money. My uncle was getting pretty drunk by then and angrily yelled at my dad that he shouldn't always bring up the subject. Then he said that my dad and mom were terrible parents because they can't control a four-year-old boy who was evil. Apparently, my cousin told her mom about the money I showed her. This angered my Dad who was also pretty drunk. I was called into the kitchen, and my mom asked me if this happened, and I said, "Yes, but I didn't take any. I didn't know it was wrong."

Few more hours passed, and my mom came to tuck me into bed and listen to me say my prayers. I was concerned that I had done something wrong, and it worried me. I overheard my aunt say that she was going to cut her wrists, and this scared me. I was reassured that everything was all right.

What I didn't know was that my dad was so angry that it almost turned into a physical fight with his brother. My dad threw them out of the house and told them never to come back. Forty years passed, and they never said one word to each other. Even when my dad died, my uncle refused to go to his funeral. They hated each other!

Other than that, I was living a normal life, with one exception. A man used to visit me almost every Sunday. I was told that I was a lucky boy for I had two dads. He would come and bring me candy and things like that, and I would climb all over him. He turned out to be my paternal father. My biological father and my Uncle Adam would spend the afternoon with drinks. I didn't really realize the relationship at the time, and I wasn't told. I just thought I was lucky. The only thing I really knew is that I had two dads.

I was about eight years old when I was told that I also had another mother. The man who used to visit me took me to one of my Auntie Katie's house to meet this mysterious woman. My dad and I were in the kitchen and I asked, "Where is she?"

My Dad pointed to the living room where a head peeked around the corner. She had short messed up brown hair, thick glasses, and looked a little homely. I wasn't sure what to make of her. I wasn't excited to see her, and was a bit standoffish. After eight years, I was supposed to love and accept this woman as my biological mother. I couldn't do that. I would call her "Mom," and be friends with her, but that close bond would never manifest. She knows that I have my limitations with her, but I really don't know what her feelings are of this.

For a few months, she lived with my biological dad on the same property in a trailer. I remember playing hockey with her on the homemade rink. I had fun and liked her, but something was missing. After that, it would be several more years before I would see her again.

The spring of that year, I took a shovel to the ditch outside our property and started digging a hole. I was obsessed with this project all weekend long. It was the length of my body and about four feet deep. At the head of the hole, I took two pieces of wood and nailed them together to make a cross and banged it in the ground.

That following Monday, coming home on the school bus, I told my friend that this was my grave and that is where I am going to die. My memory fails me as to what prompted me to think and do such a thing. I was honest and sincere. The belief was that my time had come. It felt like the right thing to do.

Till this day, I don't know what prompted me to act out this event. There was no child abuse or adultery or anything that should have set this off. The only thing that was happening at the time was that my Dad was a heavy drinker and became quite mean at times. Perhaps, I was questioning why I had two moms and dads and became confused and unable to handle the situation. I was not told the story of why I was not living with Daddy Joe. I didn't know anything about my biological mother, Rose. I had questions that were never revealed. I learned the truth the hard way. Maybe, something happened at school, I just don't know why I wanted to die at eight years old.

I remember one time we were coming home from a drunk at Uncle Johnny's in the wintertime. My mom and dad had had an argument in the truck. There was yelling going on. My mom got out of the truck. I don't remember if the trucked slipped out of gear or if Dad put it in reverse. The door knocked my mom down, and he drove over her leg. It wasn't broken, but it was badly bruised for weeks.

At the age of five, I already knew what I was going to do. While in school, the principal asked me what I want to do, and I told him that I wanted to be a soldier. This did shock him, as this can be a short-lived career depending on the world situation. This did not bother me for I knew it was my fate. I had it in my blood. I don't know where it came from or how it manifested.

It did seem odd that a mild mannered and loving little boy has chosen such a violent occupation. However, I was only five years old. What did I know?

Ever since I can remember, my mom always told me that if someone was to hit me, I was to either walk away or turn the other cheek. I have lived by those words all my life, never fighting back, even if it was my right to do so. Today, I let people take advantage of me, for I always give them the benefit of the doubt.

I never grew a backbone. I always turned away from confrontation. I'm much too kind-hearted, and I have been hurt and abused all my life because I live by those words. Never fight back. Don't lower yourself to their level. Keep your chin up and walk away like a man. That is what Jesus did, and that is what I was taught to do. Unfortunately, in today's society that rule does not apply. Maybe in the sixties, at the time of free love, it was. Today, you are dead meat. I still cannot change my ways. I was brainwashed as an infant, surrounded by isolation, love, and strong moral discipline.

I never saw violence, cheating, stealing or even swearing. I lived a sheltered life, in a glasshouse protected from the evils of the world. I didn't even know that the Vietnam War was raging on killing thousands of people. I never saw a news broadcast for the first twenty years of my life. When I did, I became severely depressed. Till this day I cannot fathom the six o'clock news.

Other than the seduction of my cousin, my first five years of life was sheltered with hugs and kisses in midst of nature surrounded by trees, blue sky, and flowers. Then I went to school and saw the evils of human nature. I was shocked to death. Bullying, hitting, fighting, swearing - and I was the target of it all. I was horrified and scared to go to school. Terrified and unable to fight back, I didn't even know how to protect myself from harm. I was a scared and frightened little boy. I never had a confrontation in my life, and I didn't know how to deal with it. Crowds petrified me. I had been used to being by myself for the past five years, and all of the sudden, I was thrown into a crowd of hostile children.

This was too much to handle. I found a rock and crawled under it. I have been a target all my life. This was reinforced every Sunday when the family would wash up and get dressed for church. There, I would hear stories of how Jesus gave up his life to wash away our sins. All we had to do was believe, and I did. Every Sunday, the priest would drive home a message in my heart that I was doing the right thing. Turn the other cheek.

Humiliated and hurt, I would gather my books and kiss my mom good-bye and go to hell. That is what school felt like. There was bullies, teasing, hitting, beatings, name-calling and I was at the brunt of it. This was a rude awakening to the real world, which I have never experienced before. The stink of urine from one girl who sat beside me in French Class used to drive me mad. Yet, I couldn't say a word against her. It was horrible, yet I kept my peace for several years. The stench was unbearable.

My religion taught me to keep peace. Later, I became an altar boy with duties to the priest every Sunday, and then there was Sunday school where the Bible was deciphered into plain language. I was taught that living under a rock was God's preference. I was doing the right thing by hiding from confrontation. When the moment arose, I couldn't fight myself out of a wet paper bag. All of those teachings buried my heart and soul further into the abyss.

I was weak and vulnerable and remained that way till this very day. The church taught me how to turn my cheek and be a real man. Today, you are forced to fight for your rights or be stomped on. These old teachings may have done well for that time for some people, but in 2005 that is not relevant. I loved my priest and cherished every word spoken. The sisters were my lifelines to freedom. They used to visit us on a regular basis and keep us in line. Even the priest would come in for lunch or coffee and see how we are doing.

We had a strong connection to the church. My aunt and uncle lived by those teachings and passed them down to me. We lived in the middle of the wilderness under the watchful eye of God.

I was taught to treat people, as I would like to be treated. I did what my aunt said and still do that today. I have very strong morals, which were buried deep into my soul. I have a kind and compassionate heart for everyone I meet. My meek character becomes a target for people who do not share my same beliefs. My Uncle Adam was very pleased with the way I turned out. He told me that I had a very kind heart, and I took that as a great compliment especially coming from him.

My uncle was very much the same way. He looked tough and worked hard, but he was quite mild mannered and loving. My aunt has the heart of gold. I was smothered with hugs and kisses all my life. My aunt and uncle were in their late forties when they took me in. People told my aunt that she was making a big mistake for she was already forty-six and taking on a six month old baby would be too difficult. They believed that taking on a baby after their own children have already grown would be too much work for their age. My aunt and uncle didn't care what people thought. They decided to bring me up as one of their own.

I was brought up in the house of love. My uncle would come home after work and do the chores and we would eat dinner in the living room as a family and watch TV. The three of us would bond together and reinforce our love for each other. Those quiet moments were just as important as work. My uncle was a proud man, and he had every right to be. He was my mentor, and I lived my life trying to be like him. Even though he had been an alcoholic, I still loved and respected him and will always know him as being my dad.

This meek and mild existence did not prepare me for life very well. I was not prepared to deal with crowds of people; I felt intimidated. I was too trusting of people and thought that everyone shared my own beliefs. I couldn't comprehend why someone would kick or punch me for no reason. I would follow the footsteps of Jesus and still get hit from behind. My teachings were not protecting me from physical harm. I really couldn't understand this, and I was very confused. I was very happy to come home at night into the safe and loving arms of my aunt.

My grades were poor, and I had a very difficult time comprehending the lessons. The atmosphere affected my learning abilities. I found it very difficult to fit in. I did find a small group of friends to play with. I felt much more at ease with small groups. I had one particular friend I was fond of. He was a little black boy, and he had a great sense of humour. He used to always make me laugh. We chummed around everywhere together. Both of us had trouble with becoming targets for bullies, but we had each other to help out in time of trouble.

There were other friends who made school life a little easier to bear. There were also a few cousins as well, so I wasn't really alone. The years went by, my confidence within crowds improved. Had I only known that in a short time this would all drastically change.

Something happened

Apparently, I wanted to live with Daddy Joe who came over on Sundays. This was not possible at the time because his life was not stable because of his work. I don't remember ever wanting to live with him, but that was revealed to me thirty-seven-years after the fact.

He was a heavy-duty mechanic for a major excavation company where he traveled a lot and lived on site most of the time. His home life was not acceptable for raising a child.

When I was eleven years old, he met this woman that he fell in love with. She was self-employed and my dad later quit the mechanic job due to a back injury. He later got married in secret, not even telling his only son.

It seemed that he now had the stable lifestyle required to raise a child. I don't remember how this all came about or the move itself, but I then went to live with my dad and his new bride.

This caused bitter feelings between my Uncle Adam and Dad. My aunt and uncle were heart broken that this event took place. The original verbal agreement was that my dad would never take me back. My aunt and uncle agreed to those conditions before raising me as their own. They didn't want me tossed back and forth causing me hardships and confusion.

Shortly after the move, I developed several problems. I became secluded in my room, only coming down for meals. I didn't go outside to play with the other children or watch TV with my dad and his new wife. I just stayed in my room staring at four walls.

My dad didn't know how to show love for me; he didn't have the slightest clue. He never came to my room or asked me how I was doing. My dad never talked to me, neither did his new wife. She already had her own children years ago. We really never connected.

They never did anything as a family, and I was never a part of their lives. I had my room and that is where I stayed for a whole year. I thought a lot about my aunt and uncle and how much I missed them. I couldn't wait till Sundays for I would go to church and meet my aunt and uncle for a few minutes before the service. I had an empty feeling in my heart; my life had drained out of my body. There was no more happiness or smiles, just a deep and dark depression. Life was in shades of black. There was no more color in my life. I was cut off from civilization, and my mind started to fade away from reality and enter a different world free from heartache and pain.

This is the second time I was able to leave reality and enter the world of darkness. There I would find solitude and peace. My mind would wander, keeping my sanity intact while in isolation. All I had were my thoughts to keep me alive. I sank like a rock. Never being able to see a light, I was consumed by the darkness.

When my father spoke, I never heard the words. If I saw something, it had no value. If I felt something, I was numbed. When I tasted something, it was bland. There was no stimulation, only darkness. My room was my sanctuary where my mind would wander off in a distance. I died once again.

Soon I developed destructive behaviour like hair pulling and cutting myself. My school grades dropped and I failed grade six. My schooling never recovered from that failure. My self–esteem was gone. I never joined in any games or activities and always stayed in a remote area of the schoolyard during recess. I was falling deeper and deeper into the darkness.

Soon, I became totally isolated and alone sitting by the fence watching the children play. I no longer had the house of love to go back to. It was all gone; it was just a memory. There was no more love or bonding. There was no love in that house, at least not for me anyway. My stepmother's most famous words to me were, "I'll rip your arm off, and hit you over the head with the wet end." I remember that quote as if it was yesterday. Those words were burned deep into my soul where they have stayed for an eternity. For a twelve year old growing up in those times, those were very harsh words. I never heard threats from my aunt or uncle; this was a shock, and it further established that there was no love between us.

Without any form of love or compassion, I sought peace and harmony in my room. My love was still on the farm with my aunt and uncle. I used to go for a bike ride on the weekends and ride to my aunt and uncle's farm, even though I was prohibited from seeing them because of a court order. I didn't know that my dad did that. According to the doctors, I was supposed to break off all past contacts with family. My father obeyed and placed a court order on my aunt and uncle. I just knew where my heart belonged. My aunt and uncle were afraid that they would get in trouble with the law. But I had to see them.

My stepmother and father ran a corner store complete with gas service. The store was attached to the living quarters in the back. This was a convenient layout for they could still have a life in the back while waiting for customers.

I was not part of the operation; they did all the work. I mainly stayed in my room even while we had guests. My stepsister would usually visit on the weekends and help out with the store. My father and stepmother were concerned about my behaviour. They often communicated with my stepsister about these problems. She suggested that it might be better if I went back to live with my aunt and uncle, but my dad did not recognize that as an option.

He sought professional help. Our family doctor lived next door and was asked to observe my behaviour. After awhile, he came to the conclusion that I should see a psychologist. Her prognosis was that I had dual personality, but I required further examination to confirm her findings.

I was then put in the psychiatric ward of the children's hospital for a six-week observation. The final prognosis was manic depression/schizophrenia. The recommendation made to child services was that I be removed from the home and break off all ties with people from my past and start fresh. My father was told that if he didn't comply with the court order that child services would remove me from the home during the middle of the night. He was forced to relinquish his custody over me to the province.

My stepsister did request to adopt me, but was denied due to her close relationship to my past. The doctor was abundantly clear that this removal from where I had grown up was necessary to my well being. From what was going on at my dad's, I was under the impression that he didn't want me anymore. I was never told of the situation or what the doctors said. I believed that my dad did not love me and that I was too much trouble for him to handle.

Within one year, I was removed from my house of love, spent a torturous year of isolation, and was put into a foster home. Yearning for my aunt and uncle, my heart and soul sank to an all time low. This was the fourth time I died.

Timid and emotionally wounded, I moved into a home of chaos. I was not used to the yelling, screaming, and the mental and physical abuse that went on in the house. There were eight emotionally disturbed children under one roof. They were dysfunctional and abused from their past lives and were congregated in one household that pretended to be a family unit.

It did not take long before these conditions scarred my character forever. There was one incident that destroyed my trust in people. Within two weeks of being placed in the foster home, the kids decided to go to the local quarry for an afternoon swim. It was a beautiful hot summer day, just perfect for a day in the sun.

There was one boy who was much older than the rest of us. He was about sixteen or seventeen. He had long, shoulder-length wavy brown hair. He seemed friendly and quiet. His character was more trusting than the other children. He called me off to the edge of the swimming hole and told me to pull down my bathing suit and bend over a large boulder.

I was shocked at his request and was trying to figure out his motive. He reassured me that he wouldn't hurt me. After some convincing, I reluctantly did what he said. I didn't see anything threatening and had no idea about erections or sex. Suddenly, I felt something go up my ass. I fought and struggled in a fury to get away from him. I was in total shock. With my bathing suit down around my ankles, I splashed my way to safety joining the rest of the children that were watching in amazement.

As I looked back, he was masturbating. I didn't know what he was doing at the time, but I later found out. My mind went blank and dismissed the carnage from memory. Very little was remembered of that fateful day at the swimming hole. That was the only time he touched me, and it never happened again.

About twenty years later, I saw a news bulletin naming a child molester who was sentenced for a twenty-year term for a lifetime career of multiple molestations. The broadcast was brief, but the name was correct and there was a resemblance to the boy who did that to me as a child. Memories rushed through me sending shivers down my spine. The details were released after twenty years of dormancy. I felt humiliated, ashamed, guilty, and hurt. I was traumatized. This was the fifth time I died.

However, this would still remain a secret for another twenty years. I was not ready to deal with those feelings at that time.

Again, I buried those feelings deep away so that they could not hurt me.

It did not take long for a mild-mannered child to make a three hundred and sixty degree turn. I didn't get along with the other children. We were all too badly damaged to have any sympathy for others. There were arguments, physical and verbal attacks along with backstabbing and manipulation. It was a large congregation of people living separate lives under one roof. Everything I was taught as a child went out the door. I was now defending my life.

At school, when I was fourteen, I became a bully, picking on other vulnerable children. I grew my hair long, down to the middle of my back. I was angry at the world. My grades were poor for I was defiant of rules and regulations. I became a troubled child. My teacher, Mrs. Dawson, was very concerned about me for we had violent confrontations. She was actually a kind soul, and tried desperately to keep the peace. Then she came up with an idea. We were mortal enemies at the time, but she picked me to stay weekends at her house to do landscaping and lawn work.

All of a sudden, my character returned back to being a courteous and grateful young boy. I worked long hours and my affection for her and her husband grew. This continued until I graduated to high school. I was no longer a troublemaker at school when I was in her class. She successfully calmed the beast.

I was going through dramatic changes. The cutting of the body and the hair pulling continued. As I was getting older, my behaviour became uncontrollable. I started smoking, drinking and experimented with drugs.

I did have some good close friends from school. I used to chum around with Albert who became my best friend and at one time my neighbour. However, I was very jealous of him. He had a girlfriend, Cheryl; with whom I fell in love with the very first time I met her. After some time, they broke up with each other.

On Friday nights, we would have a school dance. I always saved the last slow dance for Cheryl. She always accepted my offer and never turned me away. It seemed that our admiration for each other was mutual. We used to have long phone calls lasting two hours or more. She even invited me to stay with her at a house where she was baby-sitting. Somehow, I never had the courage to tell her how I felt about her.

Eventually, she got tired of waiting for me and moved on to someone else. I even asked her best friend to go steady with me just so that I could get closer to Cheryl. I regret deeply for not reaching out to her. She was beautiful and kind. Cheryl had everything a man could possibly dream for, but I blew it.

I had a couple of girlfriends after that, but my heart was still for Cheryl. Then I met a girl who had the same desires as I did. I met her at a house party, and we were deeply attracted for each other.

She was a spunky one.

I then became sexually active, and she also enjoyed the animalistic behaviour of rough sex. I would go to her house everyday after school and have sex with her before her dad came home from work. Soon, I became unattached to the foster home. I used stay at a friend's house where they would feed me and put me up for the night. I used to drink, have parties, and have lots of sex. It was a sixteen-year-old's dream come true. I only went back to the foster home for money then I would return back to the town of Selkirk. I no longer cared about school or anything else for that matter. My life there became unbearable, and it was time to move on. My world was falling apart and then I took a train to Alberta. There I stayed with an aunt and uncle for just over a year. I had a brief six-month stay with friends, and then I lived alone for six months.

So with no hope of ever finishing high school, I quit in May of 1979. Things were turning around, but I was still a shy, timid little boy. I Joined the Canadian Armed Forces. I took a bus from Medicine Hat, Alberta, to Calgary and stayed the night in a hotel, all expenses paid by the forces. Arriving fairly early in the day in Calgary, I had some time for sightseeing for I had never been there before.

I fell in love with that city. The streets, stores, and the people are amazing. I would really like to live there. I spent the afternoon and evening taking in the sights. I familiarized myself with the location of the recruiting centre, which was only a few blocks and around the corner from my hotel. I was so excited that the next day my life would change and I would start a new exciting career of which I dreamed since I was five years old. The next day, I was enrolled at the recruiting centre and a date for the course was set. In about two weeks, I was on a plane to Cornwallis, Nova Scotia, where I would commence my training as a member of the armed forces. There, I would learn the basics such as weapons training, drill, marching, physical conditioning, mental conditioning and stress management.

After three gruelling months, I survived that phase of training and was on my way to Wainwright, Alberta, for my infantry training. This was a very proud day for me for my uncle, who raised me till I was twelve years old, was also a member of the famous infantry unit, Princess Patricia's Canadian Light Infantry. I was following his footsteps, and it was an honour to serve.

However, this was not to be an easy experience, for the training was brutal, demanding, and very stressful. One thing that really stood out of my mind was while in Cornwallis was, 'The infamous sausage machine.' This term was used as you went through a large number of inoculations. We stood in a line with our shorts on and got stabbed repeatedly as we took another step forward. This was a day that we were inoculated with vaccines from throughout the world to protect us from disease when we would be called to duty anywhere in the globe. Right after this intoxicating experience, we had to run to the pool for swim training. People were experiencing the effects of the vaccines: fevers, shakes, shivers, and unconsciousness. Motor skills were inhibited causing poor judgment and a drunk like state. People were falling, bumping into things and basically needing to be rescued from drowning.

The evening was terrible, I was on the floor by my bunk wrapped in a blanket shivering to death with a cold sweat unable to work that night. There I was, huddled in a deep freeze till morning when the affects wore off. It was impossible to know which vaccine or combination made us ill. We were inoculated for dozens of diseases including Typhoid and Malaria. This was a normal reaction and was expected by the upper echelon. More than seventy-five percent of the men were ill till the next morning.

In Cornwallis I met this man who was in my sister platoon who's name was Denis. We instantly became lifelong friends.

Denis and I both ended up in Wainwright together and in the same section. It was ironic that in Cornwallis, Denis was the Most Improved Candidate. This was to also be my badge of honour when I graduated the infantry training. Before this happened, I had to grow a thick skin. The total six months of training was the most gruelling thing I had ever had to face. I was a little timid boy in a man's body. There was a time limit for me to meet mentally and physically those challenges and become a real man.

One of my greatest challenges was overcoming my fear of heights. This scared the crap right out of me. Every week, we had to go through the obstacle course, which also greatly challenged those fears. One of those obstacles was called the Confidence Tower. This was a telephone pole construction that towered up to fifty feet. It had a framework of telephone poles supporting horizontal poles spaced four feet apart from each other.

You had to straddle the bottom rung with your legs and grab the next rung and pull yourself up to do the same thing there. This would continue until you reached the fifty-foot mark where you would pull yourself up and over the top rung before descending down the other side.

The fear factor caused me to shake, shiver, sweat, and freeze in place, unable to proceed any further. For weeks on end, the tower was superior and beat me every time. Near the final weeks of training before graduation, we were up there again. This time, we had built teamwork, working as a fighting unit. I was no longer alone with my fears. My friend Denis started by cheering me on adding confidence to my ability.

I was on the tower with those same fears when soon the whole platoon was gathered below yelling words of encouragement. Denis was the loudest voice of them all. Slowly, I surpassed my usual spot where I have failed many times before. Racked with fear, I slowly continued to the top rung. This was the point of no return, either I go over the top or fall off due to my overwhelming fear. I was scared shitless; I had a drawer full of it.

Finally, shaking and squirming, I slithered over the top rung and started my decent. There were loud cheers for I had faced my fears and overcome them. The confidence slowly returned as my decent continued. I finally was on the ground and loudly congratulated by my fellow comrades. I beat that son-of-a-bitch!!

From that point forward, I knew that I successfully passed the course. That was the only thing stopping me from reaching my dreams of being a soldier, and I damn well did it! The rest was gravy.

That was also the clincher that won me the Most Improved Candidate Award for which my aunt and uncle were very proud, and so was I. I proudly followed my uncle's footsteps and became a Proud Patricia.

There were other hardships during this time such as being a victim of bullying from four evil-minded men, which would haunt my every move for my entire military career. I had rough times getting along with the aggressive bunch that used to ridicule and taunt me to no end. These bastards kept it up throughout my ten-year career, making life a living hell.

Right from the very beginning there was sneering, name calling and belittling. This would even go as far as putting date rape drugs in my whiskey causing me to lose all memory of an evening, finding myself on a mattress on the floor with the bed springs on top of me containing my movement during the night. There was also taunting and putting shaving cream on my pillow as I slept. I could not retaliate for I would end up in jail.

I wanted to kill them and if I seen them today it would take a great deal of restraint to stop me from doing so. I hate each of them with a passion. The anger boils in my veins for what they did to me and I want revenge!

The constant pranks, some of which were dangerous, left me scared and watching my back. Their irritating voices boiled my brain causing me to clinch every time I heard or saw them. It built up to a hatred for which I am deeply ashamed. However, if anyone deserved death, it is this foursome. May all four of them burn in hell!!

There were some good times as well, especially with my friend

Denis. At the halfway point of the training at Wainwright, we went on a bus trip for the weekend to Calgary to visit our Regimental Museum. The time was free for us to spread our wings with full pay cheques in our pockets. This was a break from the constant stress from training. One night, Denis and I went to the Husky Tower for dinner. This was a lavish event. We had our dinner and a few drinks, and a few more drinks, then more drinks, again more drinks until we had another dinner. We were there so long that there was a changing of the guards. We stayed until we were kicked out when they closed.

We talked and laughed, made fun of each other. We were counting the rotations of the restaurant made while we were there. We almost missed our bus the next morning; we made it just in time before being AWOL. I will never forget the great time we had together.

Now, I was legal drinking age and have acquired quite a thirst for the elixir. The drinks were affordable and there was easy access. It was a drunkard's incubator.

To handle the extreme stress of the job, many turn to alcohol to calm themselves down. This was no different for me. I did find the stress highly elevated. The job itself was very rewarding and exciting. Being an infantryman was a dream come true. My childhood visions became a reality. I was able to act out my aggression at the job releasing the fury deep inside. I was a soldier. To calm down the aggression in the evening, I used alcohol. I had to find a way to turn on and turn off the aggression at will. Although I never made a rank any higher than corporal, it was still a great job.

However, I was still cutting myself, and my behaviour was nearly out of control.

My job was to be a professional killer hired by the government. My attitude had to change. My meek and mild demeanour would not work in this situation. I could not stop the adrenalin from flowing, so I diluted it with booze.

Of course, there were other piss-ups which were common in those days. That was the only way to rid the body of the stress it had gone through during the week. We partied hard, very hard. Pay cheques disappeared over the weekend. Unknowingly, this was the beginning of my life long demise. This was my first true encounter with alcohol, and I really liked it. Now, I come to tears when trying to combat this disease.

If I only knew where it would have led me, I would have never started the stuff. Now, I am paying the ultimate price with my life.

Upon graduation, I was both a soldier, and an up-and-coming alcoholic. Then I was posted to Victoria, BC, with the 3rd Battalion Princess Patricia's Canadian Light Infantry. This was the start of my new and exciting career as a soldier.

I ate the shit right up. I loved it!! I was a model soldier who obeyed orders promptly and willingly. Soon, I was known as the, "Yes Man." I always did what I was told, no matter how demeaning the job. I was there, and I did it proudly. From picking up cigarette butts to scraping soiled toilets, I did it all with pride. When the time came to be a soldier on the field, this is where my heart belonged. I belonged in the field. This was my fate. I will live or die here as a proud soldier.

The exercises were a great learning experience where I was taught the tricks of the trade. I was qualified as a driver which gave me the added demand for my services. Then I was later qualified as a TOW Gunner and signaller. My career was on a roll. Then in 1979-1980, we went to Cyprus for a UN tour of duty.

That was one of the greatest military experiences I have ever had. It was real. It was not an exercise. We had real bullets in our weapons, and we wore flak vests and helmets everywhere we went. I was learning how other countries survived, and then there were the cockroaches and scorpions.

This was all new to me, and I loved it. Adrenalin and excitement pumped through my veins. This was ecstasy. I was nominated to work for two weeks at a Swedish outpost where I learned their weapons and drill. I worked in rotation on their outposts. They were a great bunch of men, and all had a good time.

At the Canadian Contingent, we had movies at night and kabobs. This was a great way to keep in touch with the modern world. My favourite time was my ten-minute phone call a week to my aunt and uncle. Sometimes, I had a tear in my eye and was homesick. I loved and missed them very much with all my heart.

I was also nominated for a two-week duty at the vacation centre, where all I had to do was deliver food and clean sheets to the guests. The rest of the time was mine. This was a cushy job where I would do the work in the morning and then hit the beaches, restaurants, and bars. My favourite bar was, The Old Barrel. A very nice British woman named Chris ran it. Her husband was a Cypriot named Bambos who was a taxi driver who used to drive me home at night for free. Chris had a pet name for me. She called me, "Smiley." I used to smile a lot after having a few drinks. I would stay till closing and help her clean up. It was a wonderful friendship.

I had a two-week holiday during which two acquaintances and I rented a car in Germany and traveled to France and Holland. We visited famous landmarks and museums. There were graveyards of fallen comrades to whom we paid our respects at Normandy. We also went to the infamous beach-landing site at Dieppe. Touching base with history made me feel lucky to be alive and free, for my comrades had fought and died for my freedom. I owed them my sincere gratitude.

The six-month tour in Cyprus seemed to pass very quickly. Before I knew it, I had earned my UN medal and was on my way home to start my leave. I would spend time with my aunt and uncle for a couple of weeks before returning to Victoria to get ready for a winter exercise. Although, it was a great experience overseas, it was nice to come home and see how fortunate that we really are compared to other countries in the world.

The remainder of my career consisted of summer and winter exercises and training. One summer exercise was most exciting. There was an operation code named, "Royal Concert." It was a live fire exercise that consisted of many different elements of the armed forces working together throwing millions of dollars worth of ammunition down range. There was tank and artillery support. Huey Cobra Gun ships were firing their missiles, and the jets strafed the field with napalm. The infantry supported small arms fire such as personal weapons, machine guns, TOW missiles, grenades, mortar fire, and almost everything else we had. All this ammo was being thrown down range at a rapid fire. I have never seen so much firepower in my life. Not a single insect would have survived such a blow. It was exhilarating. I must have ejaculated three times while firing down range.

Throughout my career, I was employed as a stores staff working for the CQ, re-supplying the troops in the field. Then I was the second in command at the company transport. I was also employed in signals platoon for a few years before moving to trade pioneers as a carpenter.

I loved every minute of my job. However, illness would soon destroy everything I had worked for. The army was the best thing that ever happened to me. However, my mild and nervous character had a large influence on my capabilities. I battled very hard to become the man they wanted me to become.

Magic in the Air

On a Friday night, I decided to go to the bar and get plastered. What I didn't know was that I was about to meet the woman of my dreams. I was quietly sitting down by the wall when I noticed two women walk in. One of them had the most beautiful smile I had ever seen. I instantly perked up my ears. She was beautiful! I moved to her table and talked and danced the night away.

I tried to get her phone number, but she kept on making excuses. She thought I was the same as all the guys, only wanting one thing. That wasn't true. I wanted the whole package. Her friend gave me the phone number and told me to meet them the next day. One year to the date that we met, we were married.

Kathy was the perfect choice from the start. She is kind, fun loving and gentle. She was a chambermaid at one of the leading hotels in Victoria, BC. She was concerned at first of my intent, but later realized that I really did love her. Kathy was twenty-three while I am two years younger. That little difference in age didn't matter one way or the other.

Her dedication to life is second to none. It could be a relationship or work; she will never throw in the towel. Once she makes her mind up, it will never change.

There is one day in particular that I really do remember most of the details and that was our wedding day. We saved thousands of dollars ourselves and planned the wedding without any help. We bought the bride's maid dresses, rented the tuxes, and supplied all the booze for the wedding. We supplied everything, except for the catering, which her mom and dad paid for. That is something they wanted to do.

In the morning, the best man and ushers decorated the two Lincolns. That morning my bride-to-be was at the hall putting on the final touches.

Before you know it, we were at the church waiting for my fiancée. The service was a full one-hour with communion. We felt very strong about being blessed under God. The church was beautiful and quite large. Friends from all over were there to see us get married. However, I did not have one single relative attend the wedding. I was hurt that I could not share this day with family.

I did have some of my best friends from the army come though. They were all on their best behaviour and acted appropriately. The other guests just loved them. One of those friends bought a brand new suit for the wedding and bought us beautiful fine china as a wedding gift. The maid of honour's father was in a wheel chair and even he bought a new suit to mark the occasion.

The groom's party waited at the altar for the bride's party. Her dad was a stickler for time and had her in the church precisely at two P.M. The foyer's door opened, and I saw the most beautiful woman in my life. She had a twenty-foot train that flowed like snow behind her. Lace graced her body making her glow like an angel. Everyone was at the altar, and the service began. There was a mass and scriptures, which coincided with our beautiful day.

The service went without a hitch with the exception that my fiancée's chair leg was at the very edge of the step. It was close to toppling her over backwards in the aisle. Everything else was as smooth as silk.

After being married, we went to a bird and plant conservatory for pictures. I had a single picture of myself with a pink Flamingo behind me. That was a great picture. The tropical plants and birds set off the picture just right. It was a beautiful backdrop.

It was now time to head off to the reception. The hall was decorated immaculately. The tables had the finest china and silverware. The cloth napkins were folded precisely, and the decorations set off the tables with style.

Finally, it was the moment of truth. It was time to eat. The food was fantastic! We even had lasagne, and it was a big hit. My friends went back several times for more. I was told by several of them that this was the best wedding they have ever been to.

After dinner, we danced and greeted our guests. Then we went to get changed, and we came back to party for a while. Before I knew it, it was time to go back to the hotel room. We had to get up at four A.M. We had a six o'clock flight to Winnipeg that morning.

The party was just getting warmed up when we were leaving. Apparently, the guests rented the hall for another two hours. We were in tears as we were thanking my wife's parents for everything they did for us. Then we were back at the hotel. We were exhausted and barely had enough time for anything else.

Soon after, it was time to go to the airport. My friend picked us up, and we almost missed the plane. They had to hold it for us. When we got on board, there was applause, for the Captain announced that we were newlyweds and had our reasons for being late.

After a day of traveling, my cousin picked us up, and we went to the hotel to drop off our stuff and go for dinner with his family. Right after dinner, he went to a phone and reported to mom not to worry: Kathy is just like one of us. Then as a surprise, we went to my Godparent's house for a party in our honour.

There was more food and drinks of all varieties. This was my wife's first introduction to Ukrainian and German cuisine. We raised several thousand dollars in gift money from that party. It was a wonderful time. Even my birth mother was there having dinner with my new wife. They got to know each other very quickly, and got along well.

The next day, we got some winter clothes for my wife because she was freezing in minus forty-degree weather. We did a little sightseeing; then we took the bus that evening to the farm to see my mom and dad. To our surprise, there was another dinner and party in our honour. Again we raised thousands of dollars in cash. It was overwhelming for my wife and I to have all this happen so quickly. This was our new beginning in a life together, that I have never regretted.

Soon after, my wife realized a problem and even made a

complaint of it, but I didn't recognize her concern. She mentioned that our lovemaking was basically only an action, and then I went to sleep. She did not recognize any romance. Years passed, and she lived with it until she could not stand it. She started to push me away and avoid physical contact.

I was puzzled and concerned for we no longer had intimacy. More than a decade later, she confessed that she was so distraught that she saw her doctor about it. Apparently, without my recognition, I was so rough in bed that every time we made love, I actually raped her. There was no love or romance, just hard, rough sex. We have not had intimacy for many years.

She is afraid of it, and so she rejected it and me. It seems that the problem had a huge impact on my wife for she did not know what to do. She was advised by her physician to take care of her own personal needs first and if that meant forgetting about sex, so be it.

My Personal Front

The diagnosis of the day is bi-polar depression, which is now controlled by medication. The other diagnosis is a personality disorder, which cannot be treated by medication. The doctor revealed my thoughts and past actions to me.

The connection was then realized. Understanding these connections is half of the battle when dealing with mental illness. There was a time in my life when I was compelled to mutilate my body by using a knife. There was never any thought towards those actions. It was an automatic response to my mental state. Those actions were never planned or choreographed. The injuries were, at times, severe enough to require a lot of stitches, although that didn't matter much. While committing those injuries, there was never any physical pain involved. At the precise time that the blood was dripping out of my body, I felt a calming effect that was, in fact, pleasurable.

Two years later after our marriage, while on summer exercise, I was having a difficult time with my commander. I told my superiors that I was going to lose my mind, and they dismissed it as a joke. I was drinking heavy and was quite incoherent. Finally on one heavy rainfall, I took a shovel and compass and went into the bush to make a grave. It was about five feet deep, and I covered the hole with a tarp and branches to help support the weight of the dirt. Then, when I got into the hole, I would kick the supports and have it cave in on me. Just seconds after coming out of the hole, it caved in, and I gave up on that idea. Confused and exhausted, I went back to the tent and slept it off.

The next day wasn't any better. I went for a major piss up. I got into an argument with the on duty Master Corporal and stomped off to my tent. There I wrote a suicide note to my wife and proceeded to sharpen my knife. When my tent mate, Norman came in, I totally lost it. He was not only my sub-ordinate--he was also my friend. I have good memories of our friendship. We got along very well together. We spent hours in a hostage situation. I was holding myself hostage by threatening to harm myself if he made a move or attempt to do something. We talked for hours and I was getting exhausted from the ordeal. As I was getting tired and dosing off, he ran to the command centre and alerted the staff of the situation. He came back, and I started cutting my neck, fortunately, the knife was very dull and didn't do any damage. I lost control. I wanted to die. I was so exhausted that I was straining to stay awake. After some time, I told him that I hadn't mailed the letter yet. He checked out the wounds, which were minor.

I went outside to take a piss and I took the knife with me. As my back was turned, my tent mate grabbed me from behind holding my arms down to my sides. I instantly dropped the knife, for I didn't want to hurt him. All of a sudden, the whole command centre raced out from the tent next door. From there, they escorted me to the hospital and sent me home shortly after.

I was in a hospital for almost four months. There were medication changes and observations. None of them were working. At first, the doctor was blaming the marriage. That was ridiculous. I was worse off being treated than not treated. The medication was making me ill and cloudy headed. I was attending support groups to try to make sense of all those things that were happening to me.

I barely knew where I was. However, I was released from hospital with a lot of medical restrictions that prohibited me from doing the most minor tasks. I felt useless and belittled. I was no longer an active member of the armed forces. I was categorized as unfit: driver, duties, weapons, drill, and physical training. They took my whole life away from me. My self-esteem plummeted for my dream of being a soldier was slipping between my fingers. I was put on the disabled list, and that is where I stayed till the end of my career.

The army did try to get me back into active duty by putting me back on the section commander's course. I was failing miserably unlike the same course that I took before. I failed the last course due to my mental stability; I cracked up and could no longer continue. I failed drill, tests, and lectures. Finally, it all came down to a boil. We were scheduled to have a live fire exercise the next day; the evening prior we were preparing for a mess dinner rehearsal. We were all dressed in our dress uniforms and leaving the building when the acting sergeant major made a comment about my speed. I took great offence to that remark and exploded. I spun around and screamed at him and ripped open my tunic tearing all the buttons off. I lost it. I went over the edge and threatened him to watch his back tomorrow on the range.

This caught the attention of the upper echelon, and I was placed under medical supervision. Later, I was kicked off the course and escorted home and admitted to the hospital. This incident resulted in my medical release from the military. My career was over. My life was over. My self-esteem was tarnished for I had failed. I then died for the sixth time.

My final diagnosis was manic depression upon my release. My mind brutalized me, sending my soul to the bowels of hell. I never recovered from that blow and have never been successful in getting a job since.

Luckily, upon joining the forces, I enrolled in a military insurance plan. When released with the medical problem, I was an acceptable recipient of long-term disability. Financially, I have been taken care of ever since.

Today, I learned that some people perform self-mutilation to ground themselves from slipping away from reality. It is a self-induced method of shocking one's self from drifting away into their private world. This method is used to break free from the disassociate spell and realize reality one more time.

That is the reason why it's an automatic response. The cutting of the flesh was a response to a threatening situation. This is a crude manner of self-preservation.

Once you cross the threshold and leave reality, there is no way to pull yourself back into the real world. It requires the help of others to make you realize that you are in the wrong world. It was suggested it might take a strong shake from a friend to help you snap out of it. However, some people turn explosive with rage when confronted even with minimum force. Severe violence should be expected as a possibility when awakening them back into reality. As for myself, I don't suggest this method of help. My temper can be volatile and my actions are unpredictable. Some people don't wake up as easily as others while in the grips of a personality disorder.

I was puzzled as to why I would act so strangely at times. The actual condition is called "detachment." This is when your mind detaches itself from reality. Time is the other ingredient required to help heal the wounds of such a condition.

If this is such an easy condition to cure, why have I not known this prior to now? I went my whole life with these episodes of confusion and detachment. Why didn't other health care professionals pick this up years ago? There are still a lot of questions to be answered. It may be easier to follow the doctor's instructions now that I understand what is happening to me. I feel ashamed that I could not have just shrugged off the episodes on my own without the aid of professional help.

The feelings of despair are constant. The confusion surrounds me daily. Where do I distinguish the time that I am about to lose control? This is the darkness by which my mind and soul is engulfed.

It is like an overpowering entity that controls every aspect of my life. Up until this time, I have never been able to escape the clutches of darkness. The good news is that I'm still alive. The bad news is that I don't realize that I'm alive.

I'm not even sure that being alive is such a great thing. As it is now, I'm in a state of illusion seventy percent of the time. This detachment affects almost every part of my life. I don't know how to evade detachment as described by the doctor. It isn't that simple. It is very embarrassing when friends and family notice this dazed look over my face. My facial expressions twist as if I was having a stroke. This is very noticeable and is a great concern to my loved ones. Everyone I meet mentions that I don't look well and am worried about my well being.

At this point of time, I'm already off to La-La Land. My wife does not dare wake me up from my trip while other people are around. That would cause an ugly disturbance and become too much of a heartbreak to the ones I love. It is best to let me leave reality and remain harmless than to return and be hostile. I remain in a total daze for hours, perhaps, even days. I am still able to complete tasks and chores. However, I am amazed how I can ever accomplish these tasks, especially when I can barely remember doing them.

Using power tools or machinery is an amazing task when I am unaware of what I am doing. Every little chore that I try becomes more and more difficult as time goes on. Quite literally, I am brain dead. I am unaware of my surroundings and who is around me. Somehow, I still manage to avoid serious accidents or injuries. I can't feel joy or love. I don't feel sadness or hate. I feel numbness and nothingness. I tend not to be a very welcome member at a gathering because of my demeanour. I feel nothing!

The doctor can't help me with this problem. This is something that I have to learn to achieve on my own. I don't know how. I don't even realize when I'm switching in and out of reality. The only symptom I have when I have slipped out of reality is a numb feeling in the head. I also require a lot more concentration to complete even the simplest of tasks. It becomes extremely difficult even to wash dishes because of the lack of concentration.

The length of time that I'm away from reality has greatly increased over the last month or so. I am worried if the trend were to continue, I might never see reality again. Maybe the next time, I'll never regain my consciousness of life, as I know it. How will I ever know if I just spent twenty years in a mental institution? How can I avoid this from happening?

It is no wonder the mentally ill turn to substance abuse. They usually turn to alcohol. A little bit of freedom or happiness is better than nothing at all. I could easily fall into that trap if I didn't have better priorities. It is very hard to resist such a temptation. The escape from this torture is such a treasured time that I never want to return. In other words, I just don't stop drinking. Either way, I am tortured. Of course, the best route is not to drink. That is also not as easily done as it is said.

Personally, I have been able to either exhaust myself from the condition or an outsider has been able to shock me back into reality. Usually, exhaustion will slowly defuse the situation as time goes on. It seems that after the episode is over, I feel much better. Once the body is grounded again in reality, the healing segment begins.

As a mentally ill person, I must learn to detect such events before they happen and ground myself prior to leaving reality. The grounding process is not supposed to use mutilation as a method of awakening. Throughout the years, I have never been able to predict exactly when I am about to lose touch with reality. When I lose the ability to stay in reality, there are no rules or boundaries that I will not cross. This could be in the form of adultery, rape, risk-taking, and over spending my money. Even homicide has been a swirling thought in my mind. This makes it extremely difficult to perform the grounding techniques as described by the doctor.

After detection that such an event is evident, I am to take several deep breaths and move onto another activity. The only problem is I don't realize when it's about to strike until it's too late. If I were to use the doctor's grounding methods, I would be hyperventilating until I pass out. Perhaps, a short nap would do me good.

I usually use alcohol during this time period. This may be the reason why I wasn't getting drunk during those heavy binges. I really was not mentally there. Physical pain and alcohol have very little effect while I'm in an episode. During an episode, my sexual urges go into the extreme; I stalk, stare and fraternize with beautiful women. To stop myself from this behaviour I would go to the washroom and into an empty stall. There I would lift my shirt and cut myself with a knife in hopes of stopping me from losing total control. The idea was that the pain might be significant enough to snap me out of my trance thus stopping further behaviour problems. This would also reveal why my conscience and judgment are not the same as they usually are. These normally strong characteristics are absent while in the middle of an episode. Without my normal characteristics in place, trouble or danger is not regarded as threatening. Dangers that I would normally find threatening look welcoming.

From the past, I have noticed that I don't snap out of these episodes very easily. I believe it would take some extreme force or violence against me to snap me out of my trance. Luckily, I have never been in any very dangerous situations where bodily injuries were involved. The doctor commented that if physical violence has not been evident so far, it is quite safe to say that violent tendencies will not appear in the future. However, there are no guarantees that I will not become violent.

Throughout the years, I've learned how to dismantle physical violence before it has a chance to happen. Even during an episode, it seems that I still have enough sense to avoid having a physical confrontation. I usually leave the area understanding that I cannot predict my actions while in a physical confrontation. This is a fear of mine. It is the one side of me that scares me to death. I don't know what I'm capable of doing. This is one part of me that I'm not willing to find out about. Avoidance is my salvation.

My wife is a very beautiful and very strong woman. This is just one of those things that she is unable to face. That's why I have kept so many secrets away from her.

I always knew she loved me, but this battle has to be fought alone. I knew that this is something that she would not get involved in. In her heart, she believes that I will not survive. She knows that I will not die of natural causes. I have been trying to protect her from the effects of my inner life so that I won't hurt her. I have honestly loved her and that love will always be for her.

I was very serious when I made my wedding vows to her; I have always honoured those vows. I will never sway from my word. With this illness or condition or what ever the hell it is, she is not trusting of me. After reading some of my transcripts, she does not recognize any similarities between the two lives. For her to realize what kind of challenges that I am facing is too difficult to understand. She is not willing to want to understand. It is to her best interest and her personal will to reject any conversation or relation to my mental health.

We really love each other very much. She loves me, not the evil demon that is hidden underneath my flesh. This demon seems to be very real to her.

She has witnessed on many occasions the coldness and ruthlessness that dwells inside of her husband. The total rejection that she bears towards my evil is her saviour. When my evil starts to raise its ugly head, she knows exactly what to do. She grabs our beloved pet and they both retreat to a remote area of the house until the danger has passed.

My behaviour scares both my wife and our wonderful dog. Even the dog is scared when I go through a mood swing. That reaction is my cue. If I realize what is happening, it is now time to leave the house.

I finally return when the real me is in control. The avoidance of personal contact is my assurance that I will physically hurt no one. I disappear for several hours, drink a couple of beers, and relax. I do not return home until I am able to regain control of myself. I have never physically hurt her, but I fear that I have mentally bruised her for life. Leaving the house is a safety precaution that I use to ensure that there is no physical violence. I am afraid that the mental scars that I gave my wife may never heal. Those scars that she has felt from my behaviour are something that I do not want to ever happen again. Time and time again, the same behaviour puts real fear into the hearts of my family. As much as I truly love my family, this monstrous behaviour still exists.

Financial, self-esteem and self-worth was ruined. I was no longer able to support my wife or myself. She became the breadwinner and our roles changed. My ego was destroyed, for now I was running the house instead of working for a living.

This whole time was marred by my heavy drinking habits. I would go on drinking binges and walk the streets at all hours of the night and into the early morning, not returning home until six in the AM. In many cases, I was also cutting myself at that time. I would return home bloody and exhausted which, would cause me to sleep for three days solid to recover.

These binges were triggered by my illness, during which my

alter ego would emerge. This altered state was a manifestation of my dark side, consisting of my angered and sexually hyper characteristics. I would sit in darkened corners of the bar, observing the other patrons and casting judgment on them. My anger would grow to a climax waiting for the moment to unleash my fury. Fortunately, it never came down to a physical confrontation. Somehow, I was able to restrain myself from getting into trouble.

Sexually hyper, I would scan the bar for women who met my desires. I would dance and flirt with these women. This would keep me sexually aroused. I would fall into the folds of darkness of a whole other world.

I would disassociate from reality and dwell in a world without rules, regulations, or morals. Laws were nonexistent in my world. There were no thoughts to my actions; they were just automatic responses to the environment and situation surrounding me. I may have known what I was doing, but it was not considered either being right or wrong. Those actions were validated as being the only choice and responses were made.

This particular time is when I am totally out of control. I do not respond to reason only to the situation. I cannot make a conscious decision based on reality. You are entering my world now; you play the game with my rules. My rules are that there are none; anything goes. The stakes are high and may even cost you your life. Life is very dark in here; anyone who dares enter it must be able to keep his or her eyes and ears open.

When in that state, I have no concern of my own well-being or safety. I push the envelope to the edge. Sometimes, I am the instigator of a situation. Most of the time, I am the victim. I am a very timid and vulnerable man and can easily become a target for the more devious. When consumed by darkness, my will for survival does not exist; thus, there is no reason to fight back. I am at the mercy of fate.

The darkness keeps me mentally and emotionally safe,

blocking out interference from the outside world. I am out of tune with the rest of the world. Nothing can hurt me; the worst-case scenario is that I will die and that does not upset me in the least. As a matter of fact, I welcome it with open arms. This is my sanctuary where I rest peacefully away from carnage and mayhem of your earth.

This state of mind can be magnified by alcohol. I slip away for hours at a time, blocking out emotions that would normally harm me. This form of harm reduction is much more acceptable than what can happen if I didn't drink. Although damaging as it is, this is one way to stay in control. I disappear from reality and go into the safety of darkness.

Practically incoherent to the outside world, I search for my personal gratification. I look for any form of stimuli from your world to heighten my desires. My personal pleasures are all that consumes my mind and soul. This is my personal goal. I will stop at nothing to accomplish those goals.

I magnify these feelings with alcohol, which, in turn make me a monster with no morals or acknowledgement of any other human being. Their welfare - mental, physical or emotional - has no bearing on my wills and wants. If I want something, I will wait for the right moment and take it.

Human life has no value, nor can anything human make me change my mind. If you want to dance with me, you have to pay the piper. At this point, I am volatile and very dangerous to others and myself. This is where my evils dwell.

This is my home away from home. The shadows of the night and the empty streets become my private domain. I am their friend and protector. The homeless, the hungry, the addicted, the sex trade and all the other social outcasts are my friends. They don't have anything else. At least I can give them my support and friendship.

This is where I go. My destiny belongs in the darkened alleys and corners. My psychosis has been intertwining with my life in reality. I feel the need to be close to them and be there for them. Even during the realization of reality, I feel a need to help these poor people.

During psychosis, I am drawn even closer. I talk to them, give them food, money and my friendship. I am compassionate to their needs. It breaks my heart to see these people in such desperate conditions; I wish I could do more. I feel a deep connection with these social rejects. It seems that I was put on this earth to help them. This is my calling.

The streets also belong to me. I am just like them. It is a kinship that I feel with these poor people. I have the same thoughts and feelings as they do. I also belong here. This is where I am at peace with myself. There have been numerous times that I have put my own life in jeopardy while trying to help someone else. I risk my life and the love of my family for the street life. I have a secure and loving home and family that worries and love me, yet I will still disappear during the night and onto the streets. These are tremendous risks, but they seem insignificant compared to the needs of these people.

I travel the streets numb. I feel no emotions, only my personal gratification. This also includes sex. I would entice this energy by going to the strip club. There never seemed to be enough stimulation to fuel the hyper sexual desires. I would sit in a darkened corner, oblivious to the outside world. The dancers were not enough to raise any emotion. I would sit there staring right through these women with an emotionless glare. Hours upon hours would pass, and I would still be there, alone with my emotionless calm. The darkness overcomes my soul, and I leave reality in my wake.

I leave the bar and walk the streets looking for anything that causes some sort of stimulation from my emotionless state. I look for colors or light to shine down on me to breathe life into my hibernated body. The alcohol does not elate moods or give the thrill that I seek. Many times, I don't even know what I'm looking for until something catches my eye.

Unnoticed prior to this particular psychosis in September 1999, many of my adventures on the streets were sexually motivated. Unaware of that fact, I would walk aimlessly up and down the streets in the hopes of being sexually enticed.

I was developing an uncontrollable sexual characteristic, which was later diagnosed as common behaviour for people with bi-polar disorder. No matter how common it was, it was a horrible condition that could have destroyed my marriage, caused a disease, or even result in criminal charges against me. Sex is all I thought of. Since I couldn't get it at home, I went looking elsewhere.

When not on the hunt, I would buy the filthiest pornographic magazines and ease my tensions by masturbating several times a day. Soon, this was not enough.

I needed more than pretty pictures and a hairy palm. The thoughts were non-stop; I was physically ready at any moment's notice. I couldn't stop the erections; they were constant. Every woman I saw was a potential target, not a person. I was consumed by animalistic desires for sex, not caring how I got it as long as my needs were fulfilled.

Soon, I found myself in strip bars fuelling the fire that was burning deep in my soul. After a night of drinking, I would take to the streets scanning every corner for a potential victim. Prostitutes propositioned me, but by the graces of God, I was able to withdraw from my desires and resist these tempting women. I would check out exits at bars, checking the crowd for vulnerable women who were either drunk or alone. Sometimes I would stalk them for several blocks until my presence was noticed, then I would give up the chase.

I could not control these actions. I was a dangerous man with no morals or restrictions on my actions. Something deep inside protected me from going over the edge and hurting someone. I don't know where I got the strength to resist, but somehow I did.

The doctor told me that a lot of people couldn't resist their desires and find them in trouble. There is the chance of adultery or even an action as serious as rape. I was close to doing both; I don't know how I survived.

It did not particularly mean that I wanted sex, but to calm my mood, I had to ejaculate or cut myself. Both actions bring me back into the real world and reality sets in. After that, the body reels back from the soaring heights to total exhaustion. At that time, I regain my morals and emotions and return home to recuperate, which may take several days.

My body is a road map of scars and tears. Self-mutilation is a sense of relief. It lifts me out of a disassociate state and back into reality. The pain is euphoric. The satisfaction of cutting me is intense. This release from the darkness is overwhelming, and the rush that I feel from it leaves me exhausted. With the episode officially over, I can recuperate and carry on with life until the next time.

It has been somewhat confusing as to what this is. Is it a depression, mania, or psychosis? Later in life, it was discovered that psychosis was the culprit. The big clue was the hyper sexual desires and the thoughts of a spiritual nature. It is possible that I suffered this in my teens for some of my behaviour was uncharacteristic. I didn't have many problems with the spiritual side of things until decades later.

Being trapped in a disassociated state most of my life has erased many memories of my past. I barely remember my military career at all. I only remember small bits and pieces. Perhaps my lack of memory is what I needed to survive mentally. It is true that the mind will shut off events or trauma from damaging you. As they say, "What you don't know won't hurt you." Most of my life has been a blur.

My actions were not thought of, they were emotionally driven. That is why there are no memories. My mind was altered and life passed me by. I was emotionally damaged as a child by wanting to be with my mom and dad. I would never be the same again.

Downward spiral

After my release from the armed forces, my life took a downward spiral. My dreams were banished from existence. My sense of belonging was no longer relevant. Society or my country no longer needed me. Soon, I no longer cared for my own existence--nothing mattered anymore. Without my career, there was nothing left for me.

After that, my home life didn't matter; my new job was to drown my sorrows. I buried myself in the bottom of a beer mug, not paying attention to my financial, health, or social impact of my life. I just wanted to end it all, and I would abuse myself till the end of time.

The darkness soon blackened my soul. I was alone in my own little world free from the anguish of illness and relentless failures. Here, I would sit and wait for the inevitable end.

Bouts of depression, manias, and psychosis would hurl me to the bowels of hell. I visited hell on a regular basis. My actions were uncontrollable and unwarranted. Episodes of heavy drinking, walking the streets in the early mornings, and self-mutilation were in order. Unaware of why I was doing such things, the compulsion was overwhelming yet soothing.

The dark of night and my blood flowing to the ground was exhilarating. The cuts were refreshing and highly stimulating. My clothes were soaked with blood. Many times, when returning home, I would make these discoveries of the lacerations on my body and not remember doing them. It was a pleasant surprise.

I usually never went to the doctor for stitches unless the cut was extremely deep, which occurred a couple of times. I would just patch it up myself or leave the wound open. I suffered from thousands of infections but never came close to losing life or limb due to tetanus or flesh eating disease. I believe that I have been extremely lucky. I don't usually take very good care of those wounds. They may remain open and weeping with infection for four or five months before they heal. This seems perfectly acceptable to me. Besides, what do I really have to lose except my life?

I would bar hop from bar to bar getting more intoxicated each time. I would roam the streets searching for something that I was unsure about. Stimulations were something I thrived for, but from what? I would walk around in a daze for hours, not knowing what I was to do next. I was just walking off the episode slowly until it wore itself out. Then, when everyone was getting ready for work, I went to bed.

I literally went through hundreds of episodes, of which some were suicidal. Those thoughts are still very fresh and can be acted upon at a moment's notice. There is no fear from death or harm. I accept my fate at face value.

What was it that was so tragic that it destroyed my very soul? I had a few things happen, but I overcame them, or I thought I did. They should not have had an impact on my entire life. These things happened decades ago, I should have gotten over it by now. My doctor says that I have felt bad ever since my childhood, and that I am addicted to feeling bad about myself. I think that is bullshit!

I enjoy myself much better when I'm working on my books. It lifts my spirits and makes me come alive again. Not even the booze can do that. My writing is my destiny now. It is time to move on in life and see the wonders of the world that were hidden from me when I was consumed by the darkness.

I can't let my past come between an exciting future and me. It is time to break free. However, I have still not gone full circle yet. There are pieces missing to the puzzle. I did make some progress, but I can tell that there is a lot more work to be done.

This is an excerpt from my documentation while I was psychotic. This piece was narrated by an anonymous acquaintance, detailing the bizarre account of delusions. This is off the wall and over the edge literature of my mind when I was in a state of insanity. This was a crucial time in my life for it changed me forever.

Buzz . . .Times Up!

I am a man of morals. If I were not a person of high standards, I would probably be in prison. In a normal state of consciousness (as opposed to an altered state through psychosis or impairment), religion is not as much a focus in my life, as it is when I am delusional. Still . . .

This transcript is my gift to God. As strange as the events of my life have been, I trust that He planned it that way. The forces of good and evil have been in my heart many times. At other times, my eyes were closed, and I was unable to see or feel either. I was numb. Then a very strange event happened. My occasional desires for darkness showed me the light. I invited God into my heart. He gave me the freedom of choice. He does not use tricks or traps like Satan does. This transcript is my dedication to God.

Smell the Flowers

Have you ever, "Stopped to smell the flowers," or do you even know what the phrase means? Our society, and humanity in totality, doesn't even care about our own survival. We don't care about global genocide. Nearly every species of life on this planet are raped and pillaged by man and our natural resources are being consumed at an unsustainable rate. Maybe we don't have to worry now - but what about the future? What about our children?

"Money is the root of all evil." Our greed and selfishness may be the reason for our demise. The human race has long abused the code of nature. Other species take what they need to survive and nothing more. We take what we need and then exploit what we don't, all to make truckloads of money.

The rich and wealthy often become that way by immoral

means. Hunger for money and power will be the basis for world destruction. If we could share our resources, there would not be any of the evils that plague us today. Living within what nature intended for us would leave us rich within our hearts. We do not need an abundance of money. Take what you need and nothing more. Include the necessities such as food, shelter, clothing and a little money to survive on, mix them with love and morality, and you will have a happy family that will cherish their lives. These traits would be passed down the family line producing generations of joyful, productive people. Some people do live this way, and they have happy, fulfilled lives, without remorse and sorrow. They may even have joy in their lives when nature takes back what rightfully belongs to it.

Nature has to make a major correction to right the wrongs of humanity. The only way to do this is to destroy the evils of mankind. Humanity will be wiped out of existence. We are evil. Armageddon is at our doorstep. Money and greed is the recipe that will result in the destruction of mankind. Congratulations!

At least we were thinking about the world around us when we discovered the theory of relativity. "Every action has an equal and opposite reaction." That theory relates to everything we do. Life is full of consequences. Nature knows it. Nurture a flower with love and care and it will bloom with beautiful color and fragrance, all this is within nature's cycle. Walk in the park and smell the fresh air. Admire the beauty of the mountains and the ocean; become a part of it. Be astonished at what the world has to offer.

Consider this. After driving around in a poorly maintained vehicle, you park in the driveway. If you do an oil change it may prolong the beast's life. It's cheaper to do it yourself. After the job is done, a disgusting sludge is left. It can't be left lying around, or the kids and family pet could get in it. Instead of the hassles of properly recycling it, you scan the street to see if anyone is looking and pour it down the street drain. What was that you felt-*your conscience?* You shrug it off and feel more concerned about being caught than you do about the condition of the environment.

That was a job well done. Now you go into the house and grab a coffee, cigarette, and the newspaper to relax in your favourite armchair. Upon reading the newspaper, you are amazed and dumbfounded at the state of the world. The ozone layer is full of holes. Severe storms and temperature changes threaten coastal and inland habitats. Ocean life is dying at alarming rates. Many varieties of wildlife are becoming extinct, lost to the planet forever. The government is spending millions of dollars studying climate changes but nothing is done. Disgusted at the paper, your crush out your cigarette and take a nap.

Survival of the Fittest

"Survival of the fittest," we believe that phrase only belongs to the animal kingdom. Nature is often cruel. It weeds out the weak and ill, so the strong and healthy will mate and produce superior offspring that will continue the species for generations to come. So why can't this happen to the human race? Are we so arrogant about our future to think it's guaranteed? Approaching the point at which resources are no longer sustainable, mankind teeters on the brink of over population.

Medical science is amazing but it is also an exploitation of nature. Greed, once again, is the problem. Large drug companies receive billions of dollars in grants for scientific research. Once a drug is developed to cure or control the symptoms of an illness, they charge exorbitant prices for its sale. People are kept alive, with the aid of prescription drugs and equipment such as pacemakers, longer than at any other time in our history. This is causing overcrowding in our hospitals and long waitlists for care.

Euthanasia is acceptable when life becomes too burdensome and painful for the family pet, but is not acceptable for human life. The medical system exploits its patients by keeping them alive with chemicals and equipment long past the point of no return.

The human race believes it has trumped Mother Nature's hand by prolonging life, but at what cost-the suffering of the ill or the production of super bugs?

Medical treatment would be available and affordable if we allowed nature to take its course. The chosen could die when being called. Eliminate the pain and suffering, allowing the body and soul to experience the final chapter of life.

Preventative measures against diseases would go a lot further than treating an ailment with prescriptions, equipment, and hospital care, long after illness has taken hold on the human body. Death must be accepted as a part of life. When illness is upon us, nature can be cruel. We cannot change its course. If nature were allowed to continue on its own path, there would be a decrease in many of our social problems. Poverty, over crowded jails, mental illness and most other problems would be easier to handle. Survival of the fittest would ensure that only the strong and healthy would survive and mate to strengthen the species.

Governments, industry, and technology started off as good ideas. Greed and money distracted these ideas from actually helping people. Food would be plentiful, not just in the developed parts of the world. Everyone would be able to buy a loaf of bread. All people would be wealthy and rich within their hearts and not in their wallets.

The Time for Nature's Correction is upon us

Every evil that we have committed will blow up in our faces. You should have noticed the word "nature." It has been used numerous times during this introduction. Think about what you just finished reading. Replace the word "nature" with the word "God." Can you see the relationship between the two?

Our society needs to understand what our actions have done to the world. There is not very much time left. Allow your past sins to surface and recognize your wrongs. Feel the sorrow you have caused others and God. When your heart weeps with real tears of guilt, only then can you ask God for forgiveness. You must allow him to replace your sorrow with love.

This manuscript is designed to trap the immoral and it is mastered to make them read and discover all there is about them. If you have decided to read this book, prepare to be brutalized. Perhaps you have never really read your Bible or learned its teachings. After you finish reading this, I hope you will pick up the testaments and do something for yourself. Learn about God, and learn about yourself. Welcome the end of the human race with glory in your hearts.

Patrick J. Schnerch

Recipe to Evil

At birth, you are of God's design. Your soul is pure, innocent of the evils around you. Quite likely, you were a cute child. Since we know that God can create miracles, you could have been one of his finest. This is the purest innocence of your life. From this point on, your choices and the direction you take are yours alone. At this time, God is in your soul. Your cries are only for the necessities of life. You do not have greed or hatred in your heart. Waa . . . Mommy, I pooped myself. Waa…Mommy, I'm hungry. Waa…Mommy, I need your love. This is basically all you wanted when you were a baby. I honestly hope that all your needs were fulfilled.

This is the time that corruption and the will of man take over the will of God. Actually, the most formative years of your life are from the time of conception to about the age of five. From here on, you have the foundation for your adult life. Your knowledge, fears, hates, and love, have all been established. You will carry these characteristics with you until the day you die. Your parents, family, and the surroundings that you have experienced, created many of these character traits. You could be an angel or you could be the Devil himself. This all depends if there was love, morality, and faith in God in your environment. There are other necessities of life that are just as important, such as food, water, and shelter. Without this stability in life, you may be in the midst of the most evil people in the twentieth century. They were the monsters whose table manners were not corrected when sitting at the dinner table. Physically, you may be able to survive. To become a real person with compassion and love, you need the whole package.

Even in your mother's womb, you were subject to the evils of the world. Did your mother smoke, drink alcohol, or take non-prescription drugs? Was your mother under stress in her environment? Was your father supporting your mother? Did he care for her and love her during pregnancy? Did your father smoke? Did your parents even plan for your birth? All of these factors have a powerful outcome. It all depends on what choices your parents made. Some were good and some were bad. The most important factor, was there love?

Chances are that the deck was stacked against you, even at the time of conception. Now that you are born, new evils enter your world. Permanent physical conditions already scar your small human body.

Weighing in at a hefty three and a half pounds, doctors race to intensive care with your limp body. They place you in an incubator. Your mother's lifestyle caused you to be born four months early. Basically, this is nature's way of aborting the birth. Nature knew that your parents did not deserve a newborn, nor, did you need to enter the world without a good fighting chance at survival.

You have suffered mild brain damage caused by Foetal Alcohol Syndrome. The extent of the damage will not be known until you start to develop. You have lung complications, which will likely make you suffer for the rest of your life. Your poor little body didn't even have a chance to develop properly. Your early birth was caused by a bitter fight between your parents, while both of them were in a drunken stupor mixed with a cocktail of drugs. Tempers flared, and your father kicked the shit out of your pregnant mother. She just could not handle nine months of abuse. *Her body rejected you.*

After six months in the hospital, the doctors release you to your mother's care. Death was at your doorstep several times, but medical science came through and allowed you to live.

Now that you are home, you can start to develop new evils. These evils will become your character make up. What happens to you now, will become who you are. Your thoughts, emotions, and actions for the future have already been planned for you. All of this happened in ten months. You are fucked.

The cute toddler will now learn the standard of living. This is the lifestyle you will live and learn in. You won't be exposed to anything different for the next five years. You will soon accept the mannerisms and characteristics of your parents. The environment will have a severe impact on you. This could be a healthy and loving environment where you can be taught about the best things life has to offer. On the other hand, it may be selfish, greedy, and actually a dangerous environment to learn and grow in. This will be carried on to your children if you decide to take the same path. It is a very easy concept that does not require a lot of brainwork. Everything you expose your children to will cause an impact on them forever. This could be in the form of good or bad.

Let's go back to the poor baby. The surroundings are not in this toddler's best interest. Remember the baby's past. It will always have an impact on how it views the environment. From this point forward, we will give this child a name and sex. Born a male, he will be known as David. This will allow David to tug at your heartstrings, allowing you to love or hate.

Shortly after arrival home with her new bundle of joy, Karen already notices that something is wrong. All mothers notice complications, whether they are a good or bad parent. Karen notices that David doesn't acknowledge her as his mother. He seems distant and unresponsive to her voice or gestures. Puzzled at her son's behaviour, she lights a cigarette and pours herself a whiskey. She sits down and studies David who is in the playpen. From a distance she observes that he has limited interest in his surroundings. He has this blank stare that sends a shiver down his mother's spine.

Now, Karen is really rattled. She nervously butts out her cigarette and lights a joint. Hastily, she pours herself another whiskey. Shaken by her son's icy stare, she screams, "What the hell is wrong with you, you little shit?" David doesn't respond to her screams. Not a cry or the slightest response. This time while pouring her drink, her hands are shaking and unable to poor cleanly. She carelessly spills her sacred nectar. "Fuck off and die, you little shit!" Barks the staggering mother. She plops down on the couch like a bag of doorknobs. The drinks are taking affect, and Karen is more at ease. She doesn't even realize that she has a son anymore. Soon, the bottle replaces the glass of booze in her hand; Karen's world is now peaceful. She lies down and quietly passes out.

The same thing happens everyday. The house is an absolute mess. Pizza boxes with a stench of rot and a layer of maggots litter the entire house. House cleaning has never entered her mind. Liquor bottles are strewn everywhere there is room. The stench of urine is unmistakable. Karen has a little problem controlling her bladder when she is in a drunken state. She is also incapable of washing her own clothes.

Oh yes, little David is alive; however, he isn't doing too well. His condition is worsening; he is losing too much weight. A horrible cough interrupts his gasps for air. His skin has a yellow hue that clashes with his sunken eyes. One more time, nature is calling for David. Through the graces of God, David will survive. This was due to the complaint of a neighbour. After retching from the stench of passing Karen's residence, she grew concerned. The police, child services, and a team of doctors scramble to save the little boy's life.

What Constitutes An Action Being Evil?

Although this is an extreme case, even worse has actually happened. How much truth was there in the past few paragraphs? Has anything like this actually happened to someone you know? Was there any evil involved? Perhaps, David was nothing more than a victim of an incompetent mother. What constitutes an action being evil?

David was very young. He will not remember these events when he gets older. How would this possibly affect him as an adult? These events couldn't possibly have an affect on him later in life. Could they? Ask yourself these questions and you decide on the answer.

In nature, animals eat when they are hungry and sleep when they are tired. The young cuddle to their mother for love and security. They play with their siblings for a little fun and excitement. They watch their mother and copy her actions. This is how they learn survival skills. If the little ones live to reach adulthood, they will mate and continue the cycle of nature. That's it, that's life in a nutshell. Why is it so different for humans?

We find pleasure in things that will harm or even kill us, instead of those things that will help us grow to be healthy adults. Karen poisoned her life and the lives of those around her with booze and drugs. Little David's life was blighted by her selfishness.

Nature is maybe the guide to our salvation--especially if there is no other guide to follow - but will we listen? Wildlife on television's nature channels may be more moral than the human beings they share the earth with. If you don't want to read the Bible, try the monthly wildlife magazines. In North America, the native community studied nature very carefully. Their entire belief is based on it. They are a strong and proud people who have suffered immensely over the decades.

This Emotionless Child . . .

Karen did not demonstrate motherhood at its best. David has recovered, at least physically. Child protective services have placed him in a foster home until a next of kin is notified. It is unlikely that Karen will see David any time soon. Just less than twelve months old, and his ambition and happiness as a baby are absent. He is not progressing at the speed of an average child his age. There have been no smiles, attempts to stand, or even any crying. He only stares into empty space. This emotionally vacant child has become a grave concern to those who are trying to help.

The foster parents have tried several methods to stimulate David. All has failed. Bonding cannot be established because no one can enter his world. What will happen to David? How can he be so scarred? At his age, he doesn't even demonstrate a will to live. Babies shouldn't be like that. He is too small to feel the affects of his short past. Perhaps nature should have taken its course. If he had died then, the little guy would have avoided all that was yet to be.

Man interfered when God was going to take David to a better place. Even nature's perfect plan was defeated. David lives. What do you think his chances are to grow and become a respectable member of society-or even a reliable young man? God knows more about David than we do. And still, we repeat our mistakes.

You don't believe in God. He is just a belief that artificially feeds morals and love into empty hearts. Then why not believe? You may enrich your soul and become a better person. Even artificial belief is better than an attitude of superiority. We don't need rules to live by, you say, we can make our own choices and progress. Then why are there drive-by shootings, sexual assaults, and murders? Why cheat on your wife? The Holy Bible is all about the laws of nature. Go against them-rape and pillage the earth-and watch a wall of mud consume your home and everything you hold dear, simply because a contractor with a lack of vision cut down all the trees on the slopes above you. Or a storm so fierce it leaves death and destruction in its wake. Or a virus so resistant it causes a plague . . .

Karen's Bibles were the grocery store gossip magazines. She took great pleasure in reading them. Learning a better way to live did not interest her. She was happy just the way she was.

Messages from an Altered State

The following text is unedited. It demonstrates the thought processes of someone in full psychosis. Each thought was written as it came to the writer. The psychotic thoughts are written in italics for the clarity of the reader.

Days were spent at the computer. Rage and outrage are present. It may be difficult for you to read, as the thoughts are fragmented and often, therefore, incomplete. The mind becomes literally bombarded by unwanted images and ideas. Read on, if you dare.

The Ten Commandments seem to coincide with nature. You don't have to break the commandments to survive as a race. It serves no purpose to kill a human or cheat on your wife. The behaviour does not benefit us to survive as a species. Selfishness and greed are the sole reason. That's why! We do this crap just to satisfy ourselves.

The laws of nature are basically what the Holy Bible is all about, nothing more. They are interesting short stories that reflect the consequences that occur due to our greed and selfishness.

It demonstrates very cleverly to respect and love everyone and everything, including us. That shouldn't be all that difficult to grasp. So why can't we believe? It seems that if we did, it would do us more good than harm. It does not matter who really wrote the scriptures. Even if the stories are fictional, it does not matter. If the interpretation of the person who deciphers the writings is accurate, it is not of any real importance. It is important if a man rapes and murders a woman in front of her children. It is important that we don't tolerate that shit anymore!

The best way to accomplish better behaviour is through education. The Bible is your textbook. When I mention the Bible, it means in relation to any of the recognized religions. This does not include the self-righteous cults. The stories and the names may all be different, but they all believe in morality and love.

None of these religions praise violence and bloodshed. They do not accept the countless evils that are committed every day. Any recognized religion is a good religion. Anything that teaches the difference between right and wrong is a benefit to those who believe. There are a lot of similarities between them. To designate which religion tells the truth is wrong and unwarranted.

What is God? He may be a she or something in between. Possibly it is a false belief with no substance at all. Maybe, it is a spiritual force residing in the clouds in a place called heaven.

It could be an idol that only brainwashed religious freaks to believe in. There is no such thing as heaven or hell. God and angels or the Devil with demons are nothing more than a silly concept. You live; you die and become maggot food, the end. There is also a concept that the earth possesses all three dimensions.

Thoughts and emotions demonstrated here often contradict themselves producing confusion. The ageless question is there a God or isn't there, torments the mind. Such ideas may intrigue the healthy mind, or may not be given a second thought, but here they consume the psychotic mind.

The beautiful mountain range in the distance soaring through the clouds may be heaven. When we see nature at its finest, we even mention that this is God's country. Your conscience that alerts you of a bad situation may be your own. It may also be God or the spirit world trying to guide you to safety. The temptation to fill your greed and selfishness could be a communication with the Devil.

Possibly, it may be demons tempting their will on you. On the other hand, this may just be who you really are. So far, we have dealt with several ideas that become the make up of evil. Is every non-required deed, also a sin? Actually, it is. A sin is an action or deed that is not required for your growth or betterment of your species. Nature and God are very closely related. In fact they may be one and the same. What if nature, God, and the Devil were closely related? Here is something.

As the psychotic mind obsesses over the thoughts going around and around in it, more evidence is found to support its ideas, and like a hurricane it literally feeds on itself.

Issues from everyday life are swept into the funnel to fuel the writer's concepts.

Consider nature to be the confines in which God and the Devil both reign. Insurance companies use a favourite clause to bail them out from claims that have been filed. "An act of God," is their way of wiggling out of a contract. Some people believe that is bull. God wouldn't kill innocent people. The Devil would kill. The landslide swept away several homes, killing eight people. The insurance company says, "Sorry, we can't help you. It was an act of God." No, it was the act of an evil developer. He raped and plundered a beautiful forest to make way for resort homes. Even though there was no demand for such a development, the plan went through, and the developer got rich. Eventually, the homes were built and sold. Everyone knows that when you uproot trees, the ground becomes unstable. The root systems held the hillside in place in the heaviest rainstorms for centuries. The trees were removed to accommodate the new homes and landscaping.

With the developer's greed for more money, his dream became a reality. The people's homes and lives that were swept away were not innocent. They had their own greed. The homes that they had prior were more than suitable for their needs. They wanted something bigger and nicer. They bought into the developer's dream. They didn't have the slightest concern at what would be the cost to the environment. God would not kill, not even for what they did. The Devil shares the same realm as God, which is also nature. Nature fought back with a vengeance. The people who had greed and selfishness in their hearts caused all of this. The Devil stepped in and took what was his. When we throw dangerous chemicals into the ocean, species die.

We do not think when we engage in sex just to fulfill our pleasures. The consideration that you may be responsible for countless deaths seems unreal. When we drink and drive, the consequences do not enter our mind. Temptation draws us over the threshold. The Devil has us in his realm. All your actions don't go by unnoticed.

Nature fights back. AIDS kill thousands of people each year. It disrupts other lives and families at the same time. Drunk driving also does the exact same thing. The sea life dies, depleting our food source. These actions are shunned by nature. The Devil walks in behind and captures your soul.

War, that's a good one. Do you think this is what nature intended for our survival? You dumb shit! This is not the way to get along with your neighbours. Nor is it a good way to make friends. It does the exact opposite of what we should be doing. Poor Lucifer busts a gut every time blood is spilled in vain.

Powerful sexual desire is present and in many cases has to be controlled with medication. The psychotic's self-control may be lost during an episode. A normally shy, soft-spoken, and moral person may have sexual or violent thoughts that could easily be acted upon. Many sufferers refuse to take medication because it destroys their ability to perform sexually or achieve an orgasm.

Self-medication through the use of alcohol or recreational drugs exacerbates the situation landing many mentally ill patients in jail.

His tools are the addictions to all foreign substances and behaviour that is not required to promote life. Addictions to drugs, alcohol and sex are his tools. When these tools enter your mind and soul, they replace your own thought and judgment with evil. This allows the Devil to do the thinking and judgment for you. Quite likely, you have experimented with drugs or alcohol at a party. With the excitement, you may have indulged too much into your pleasures. The next day, your friends remind you of your outrageous behaviour that you performed. The things that you committed the night before were so horrible that you cannot believe that they are telling the truth. You would never behave that way if you were not stoned or drunk. Your mind and conscience were replaced by the Devil. You allowed him in, even though your conscience warned you not to take that eighth drink of whiskey. You did it anyway.

Now, you realize that you became horny at the bar. You wanted a little action. As you staggered around the bar, you saw a beautiful woman, which heightened your interests even further. You didn't even consider that her date would not allow you to have your will. Your personal pleasure had to be fulfilled, no matter what the costs. Your mouth started to flap, and then you decided you wanted to beat the hell out of her date.

The bouncer quickly removes you from the premises. Of course, this was not enough to warn you to go home. You were pissed right off! That jerk in the bar is going to get it. Besides that, your penis is so hard that it is busting through the zipper. You were not about to have that jerk screw the whore, you are!

You stood in the shadows nervously waiting for the couple to come out of the bar. You stalk them, waiting for the right moment. When the time arose, so did you. The power you unleashed on this poor unsuspecting man left him with no chance of survival. His body is bloody and limp. Your attention is now on the young woman whose life you have just shattered. The brutal rape was pure evil. The horror was intensified by her screams for her life. Even her life, you would not spare her.

It is important to understand that the above situation did not actually occur. Still, it is thoughts like these that can lead to crimes committed while experiencing uncontrolled psychosis. The power of such ideas cannot be under estimated, they can take over a normally meek demeanour, and fuelled with booze and drugs, land the mentally ill person in jail. Not all psychotic episodes involve violent thoughts, nor do all psychotics have such images.

It is interesting to note, that the writer's psychosis improves later in these journals. When on the new antipsychotic medications, and through more effective therapy he becomes more concerned with day-to-day life, and less focused on religion, God, and Evil.

Patrick J. Schnerch

Spooks and Ghosts

Throughout our lives, we have been bombarded with ideas of ghosts and spirits. Some people believe, while others do not. Television, movies, and literature have shown us spirits and ghosts in many forms. For you who don't believe in God, you couldn't possibly believe in any form of spirits.

You say you believe, but to what degree? Do you see appearances of the dead, hear noises, or see objects move by themselves? If you do, the best advice is to go see a doctor. The term they use to describe these happenings is "schizophrenia."

Schizophrenia is often confused with multiple personality disorder. The patient is thought to have a split personality. This is not true. A schizophrenic may be paranoid or suffering from auditory or visual hallucinations, but they do not have two or more personalities within them.

They may become psychotic and seem unresponsive to outside stimulation, like little David did in chapter one. To the schizophrenic, the experience of psychosis can be a form of detachment from his or her surroundings. They may be aware of what is going on around them, or they may not. The sensation of actually having left the body and observing it and the environment around it, from a distance, is an example of detachment.

Active imaginations and the personal will for such things to happen do play on your mind and make you believe that it is real. This is not to say that there are no ghosts or spirits, just in what capacity do these entities exist?

Spirits are not only possessed by the dearly departed, they can also be the not so dearly departed. When you have a thought of dear Aunt Bertha from many years passed, these memories enter your soul and open a communication link with her. Basically, you allowed the memories of Aunt Bertha into your heart. You re-live the fond relationship that you shared in the past. You also think of the relationship you could still have if she hadn't passed away. During your communication, you ask questions. In your heart, you will always feel an answer. You have allowed Aunt Bertha's fond memories to lift your own spirits. You keep her alive in your heart forever. This is what a spirit really is. Those thoughts of people dead or alive are the link to the spirits in your heart.

What are thoughts, and where do they come from? Do sane people just have different thoughts than insane people? Are their minds less cluttered? It has long been suspect that positive thinking leads to good things in life.

Perhaps the sane person is able, in some way, to let go of the thoughts that enter their mind, whereas in the psychotic mind the thoughts persist and go around and around, becoming increasingly bizarre.

Unfortunately, even the evil has spirits. There are also some hate groups and others who have accepted the spirit of infamous dictators in their hearts. They are taking over where those monsters have left off. They are basically re-living life as they want it to be. They spread hate and act out violence against minorities. They murder these people just because of their color or belief. These people have an open communication with the soul of these monsters. They have formed a bond between the spirit world and the living world. They worship them. They celebrate birthdays, dress in military uniforms, and copy every idea and mannerism they had.

The fight between good and evil continues in the mind of this individual. Days pass, hygiene, food and sleep are expendable, and within, the oldest battle known to man, is fought in his tired, vulnerable mind. Mental illness is exhausting.

There once was a man whose bond to God was so powerful that the words of God filled this man's heart and soul. When Jesus spoke, the words of God were heard. His soul and life was dedicated to teach people love and morality. This man did not show hate or anger to anyone. God was in his heart.

He spent his short life teaching others God's will. He taught us to have mercy on others and not to judge those who don't believe. He sacrificed his life. He did this knowing that the word of God was the truth. Only love and mercy filled this man's life. He felt God and knew that those words would be echoed for centuries. God lived in the heart of Jesus. Spirits are as real as you or I.

Only God has the right to judge.

Maybe . . . the sane could learn from the insane.

The stage is set; there is no way of changing it or a way to avoid it. This is not a sad time or a time to feel sorry for you. This is a time of celebration. Victory belongs to God. Evil is very powerful, the exception being it cannot enter our souls when they belong to God. The glorious day is arriving when evil will be wiped off the face of the earth. The earth will have one thousand years of peace, love and glory. It will be totally free of evil.

The angels will sing; glory will be to God. Imagine, one thousand years of no evil presence on earth at all. The world will be totally free. There is a little drawback to that part as well. There will not be any human presence on earth for that same amount of time. After that time, evil will return to earth again. Perhaps, the next human race will be a lot smarter than we were.

During this one thousand year period, nature will be allowed to recover from the sins of man. Old growth forests will return, all animal life will return to healthy populations. The oceans, air, and ozone layer will have time to repair themselves from the damage we caused. The Garden of Eden will be ready for the next set of contestants. When nature is back to its original beauty, man will return to earth again. They will never find any sign of civilization before them.

The earth will not bare any evidence. This will allow the new earth to make its own choices and find God. History will start again. The date will be 4000 A.D. Time will start over. Inventions will be built again, just by a different name. Possibly, this time as the new human race strives for existence, God will be in their hearts. This time around, greed and selfishness may not seem as important as they did to us. Possibly, after the earth is burned to the ground a few times, humanity may just get it right.

The idea of Armageddon is not new, but it is popular in today's cultures throughout the world. Some religions are based on "the end of the world" philosophies; others promote "holy wars."

Modern literature is ripe with speculation. There is often a fine line between insanity and brilliance.

It is not difficult to understand how this issue could permeate the awareness of mentally ill individuals and cause them much grief. It's all around us. The weather is becoming extreme. Lives are being lost because of storms and floods. There is a hole in the ozone layer. The mentally ill and or addicted are among the most vulnerable in society and perhaps the most impressionable. Either way, the deluded mind churns and churns, in extreme cases acting out its thoughts.

The Devil's Infliction

This is something of great interest. You cannot hear, smell or taste it, but it's still there. Sometimes you might think of it as being a little off the wall, or even absolutely mad. It is a gift from the Devil himself to all of humanity. The medical system in more developed parts of the world is still unable to treat this infliction satisfactory. It may not really be an illness at all. Maybe, it's just a character defect. Of course, that must be it. There had to be a reason for an eight year old to cook up his favourite meal of road kill. His character is just a little off.

Massacres at high schools and the murder and bloodshed are just good old character building. The manly thing to do is to have pistols and rifles in every room of the house. The stack of mercenary magazines and a revolver in the baby's nursery are good building tools. Finally, a beautiful moment to remember, little junior kills and dissects a neighbourhood pet.

These are treasured moments in today's society. You fuck'n idiots think that's funny or creative writing? This is the damn truth!! There is nothing funny about little junior stalking the house, while the family is asleep, with a commando knife in hand. Thanks to all of the mercenary magazines, he was able to use stealth to gain entry into each room and kill every one of them without making a sound. He even cut his ten month-old sister's throat. It was just like killing the neighbour's cat; there was no remorse or sadness. Now, the morning was upon him. He doesn't want to be late for school. With his family's dried blood on his hands, he butters his toast and makes his cereal. With his breakfast in hand, he wanders into his parent's bedroom. He slides up in between his bloodied parents and turns on the television for his morning cartoon ritual. Not even aware of the soils on the bed, he eats his breakfast watching his favourite show.

Upon leaving the bedroom after breakfast, he wishes his parents to have a nice day. It's just like any other day. Just as he passes his baby sister's room, he stops and turns around. He kisses her cheek and puts her favourite pink bear under her lifeless arm. As he comes to his older sister's room, he stops to piss on the door. Picking up everything he needs for a heavy school day, he leaves the house.

Is it better media coverage or maybe overpopulation? Or does it seem that more and more people are acting out their aggression. Even things like road rage are becoming common in today's society. Whatever the cause, anger and aggression are soaked up by the public during the evening news broadcast, and we are becoming more desensitized. It is the mentally ill who are most susceptible. Not necessarily because they would copy or act out their aggression, but because of those obsessive thoughts that keep revolving in their tortured minds.

Thank goodness it was just a character defect. It might have been worse. He was such a good boy. We just don't understand how this could happen to such nice people. They were quiet though. The parents worked at good responsible jobs. They loved their children and provided everything for them. We just don't understand. How can such a horrible thing happen next door without us noticing that something might be wrong?

The writer's use of sarcasm to emphasize his outrage at society's indifference is apparent in this paragraph. How can we not notice, in spite of our hectic lives chasing the dollar signs that something so wrong is brewing in our own homes and neighbourhood?

He calls it The Devil's Infliction. Perhaps he's correct. It is one way of explaining such aberrant human behaviour. A child possessed. Once again it demonstrates a mixture of reality and obsessive thinking that results in outrage to an otherwise docile demeanour.

Open your hearts to God; he will lead you to aid others. You will see the signs and hear the cries. To save a life is not always that difficult.

The Power of Insanity

Most mentally ill people feel dead inside and are already living in hell. My temptation lies within my illness. I, too, struggle daily between the two entities (good and evil). It is my hope that my morals and beliefs are strong enough to withstand the overpowering will of temptation.

When you lose control of your mind and soul, you stand alone. Morals and legalities are no longer restraints of your thoughts and actions. Instinct and impulsive behaviour is the new powerful realm that you must defend against. Without your mind and soul, you then become Satan's pawn. His will is your reaction to a situation. You are out of control and there is nothing you can do to stop it.

The writer begins to take us on a bizarre journey through psychosis and depression, where he relates to the lives of those who frequent the streets of the inner city late at night. He puts his own life at risk and leaves the comfort of his home and family, to wander from bar to back alleys, and on to other bars. Here he self-medicates with alcohol, setting up a strange ritual that robs him of all structure and meaning in his life.

The drug addicts, pimps, and hookers all need me. They need assurance that everything will be all right. The homeless need food, and I give it to them. The hookers have children and are starving. I give them food and money. The drug addicts need a friend, and I am there for them. They are all dying a slow but sure death on the streets, they have no one, and I am their protector. I'm the only one that cares if they die or not. The darkened streets are my home. This is where I belong.

In all actuality, the writer has a secure home with a loving wife and a large dog. They would not want to see anything happen to him. Still, he leaves his bed when his wife is sleeping to wander the streets. Delusion tells him that he is needed on the streets and grandeur convinces him that he is their protector. A lack of proper treatment in this instance fails to keep him safe from others, but mostly, from himself.

I watch the poor suckers who don't have the smarts to resist a come-on by a prostitute. They leave through the back door. The guy comes back a while later with a big glow. They think they are God's gift to women. They smooth talk the highly intoxicated women into seduction. The drunk or stoned pimps stagger around trying to promote their highly diseased ladies to the patrons. Under the table dealings are a common sight. The activities include drugs, stolen items, or other evil dealings.

The psychotic mind can be acutely perceptive - literally absorbing the surroundings through the skin. It can focus on the smallest action or detail while maintaining an awareness of other goings-on from a distance. It is almost like a force field around the body picking up and assimilating incoming data.

My skill at watching these people has taught me how to detect under cover officers at great distances. They can never blend in enough to be convincing. They are usually the street crimes unit. Sometimes, it's special investigators conducting leads on drug cases or busting up prostitution rings. They stand out like sore thumbs. They stink like a cop.

Heightened perceptions may be nothing more than acute paranoia or vice versa. The paranoid mind links things together to support its theory. It often feels persecuted.

When you are in bars like this, it is a lot of fun picking out who is mentally ill. You look for males between thirty and fifty years old. They sit alone, usually in dark corners or near the exit. You can watch their eyes. They are emotionless and they see everything. They are always quiet and never bother anyone.

They usually sit and drink until closing time. They are in control of their drinking habits and don't usually get too drunk. Of course, they are heavy smokers and will always have two packs on them. They look like stone statues sitting in the distant fog, very quiet and always alone.

They are deep in thought; I can almost hear what their eyes are saying. The stories on their faces tell the sadness and disgust of what they have seen. It seems we can detect the presence of others who have the same problems as ourselves. It is almost an open conversation without talking.

They know that I'm screwed up, and I know that they are screwed up. Our actions are almost identical.

At times, perception is heightened and sharp while at other times the mind is clouded and barely aware. The mentally ill person can be so confused that he can only sit and stare into space. It is difficult to think clearly enough to string actions together to accomplish even a simple chore.

This may be the side effects of high doses of medication, or perhaps a result of the actual disease, a chemical imbalance in the brain. The untreated mentally ill mind is a mind that often works on impulse and reaction instead of thought and emotion.

I suffer from severe confusion and commit acts without any thought. Possibly, this is a side effect of the medication or the lack of. This has left me with several physical complaints. The symptoms that I experience seem to nag on my conscience for days. It's like a natural instinct or calling to the dark side. The days prior to an episode leave me agitated, highly nervous. I am constantly trying to fight the battle to stay in control. From experience, I have learned that during an episode, I go through a complete character transformation.

During this time, my character is totally opposite to what I am. Normally, I am a kind, gentle, and loving person with an easy-going attitude. During an episode, I am angry and hunt for an excuse to fight or cause a disturbance. My morals and conscience are totally nonexistent. It feels that there are no rules or regulations that can hold me back from what I want to do.

I feel a strength in me that makes me feel invulnerable. Most of the time, these feelings are never released into physical action. Somehow, I am able to control myself from acting on those feelings. I am amazed that I have been able to withstand such a powerful tempting force. It is a high stakes gamble.

The writer is fortunate that he is able to analyze his own behaviour and control it to some extent. Many psychiatric patients are unable to recognize an episode. They wander the streets bewildered, unaware of their own symptoms and often unwilling to access help. They may refuse medication. Often they come to be used and abused by predators. Many mentally ill people slip through the cracks.

Perhaps, society is a little misguided in the information they receive. I tend to agree with that point. You rarely ever hear the real truth. You have to feel the truth for yourself. The truth is always inside you. It is up to each one of us to access the truth within and use it in our daily lives. As brutally honest as these transcripts are, my truth is not particularly your truth.

February 2000

That represents a small portion of the material I recorded while in psychosis. I have never had thoughts or feelings like that at any other time in my life. I was aware of something strange happening, that's why I documented it. Something told me the experience should be chronicled.

When my psychiatrist saw the manuscripts, he confirmed that they were the writings of a psychotic. He then prescribed a new drug. This is a common medication used on Alzheimer patients to stabilize their moods. The very next day, after the first dose, the writings stopped and the behaviour problems were contained. The psychosis was officially over.

A two-year depression, during which I was often bedridden, followed. All I did was sleep and drink booze. During this time, I gained sixty-five pounds and became a serious alcoholic. My muscles deteriorated to a point where my back could not support my upper body while I walked. My leg muscles were so weak that I had to take several breaks just to walk a few blocks. I was mentally and physically battered down.

I slowly recovered from the depression but not the alcoholism. I started into a mania during which, again, I had a compulsion to write. This time it was a four-hundred-page fictional crime drama. This was also written with no apparent thought. I was just as surprised as the reader to find out what was happening on the next page. Frantically, I wrote every day for nine months. A further six months was spent editing it. In November of 2003, it was published. My mania then ended and my mood stabilized.

Patrick J. Schnerch

Death and despair

I have to look deeper for there are more stories to tell. In 2000, my Uncle Adam was diagnosed with Non-Hodgkin's lymphoma. In a matter of nine months, he dwindled down to nothing. He was experiencing trouble with his heart, diabetes, and emphysema and the cancer.

Near Christmas, I decided to spend time with my aunt and uncle over the holidays. I thought that he was quite ill, and I didn't know how much more time he had, so I wanted to spend together what might be his last Christmas.

I didn't have enough money for my wife to come along on this trip, so I went alone. Upon arrival, about a week before Christmas, I opened the door to my aunt's apartment to find out that she just finished putting him back into hospital. Apparently, he'd become very sick again.

That night, I went to the hospital after visiting hours to see my dad. He was ninety pounds soaking wet. Before his illness, he weighed well over two hundred. He was very weak, but he was extremely happy that I had come to see him. He was disappointed that my wife was not there. My dad really liked her, and they got along beautifully. He missed her.

I held my dad's hand and let him know that I would always be by his side. He took that comment and held it dear to his heart. Days were passing by, and he was getting worse. He could no longer sit in a wheel chair without getting ill. He had to lie down. I visited him twice a day because my aunt was also ill at home with a heart condition. She couldn't visit as often as I could.

I would feed my dad at meal times and give him some support. He missed mom. Sometimes, he would hear her voice even though she wasn't there. About two days before Christmas, my dad and I had a very compassionate talk. He reviewed his thoughts on my life and mentioned that every thing turned out for the best when I met Kathy. He praised me for my kind heart. I was taken back by this conversation for I felt this would be his last chance to tell me how he felt. I told him for the first time in my life that I loved him. In return, he also stated the same words back to me. I have never heard him utter those words in my life.

I felt closer to him that day than any other time in my life. The hip bonded us. He was sincere and honest, and I felt his soul touch mine. Unfortunately, he was still getting worse, and the doctors ordered another blood transfusion. However, this time it didn't perk him up like it had before.

The day before Christmas, my cousin Dave and my mom visited Dad. The nurse came in and compassionately told my mom that he was dying. He may only have a couple more days left. My mom was shocked. She didn't even consider for a moment that he would not get better. She took the news very hard. My mom was oblivious to the fact that he was very ill; she thought that he would bounce back into her arms like so many times before. She was in denial.

Christmas morning, the three of us were back around his deathbed. He was barely coherent and was slipping away slowly. Our priest was making his rounds visiting patients and came to Dad to see if he could be of service. My dad readily accepted and took communion and God's blessing. We were crying for it was a sad time. My dad was welcoming God as his saviour and accepting his fate. He made peace with himself and God before traveling onto his journey home.

The whole family visited Dad throughout the day for this was Christmas. There were many tears that day, and Christmas would never be the same. My uncle left his mark on my heart. Even on his deathbed, he still recognized me and was pleased that I was also there for him.

December 26th, 2000, at 9:15 PM, Central time, Uncle Adam died peacefully in his sleep. Although it was hard to let him go, I was grateful to God for allowing me this opportunity to be with my uncle when he needed me the most.

My aunt was most gracious that I was able to be there for them both. She thanked me several times for my efforts. She didn't think she could make it without me being by her side. I was also grateful that I was there for the funeral. The family was highly distraught. I did write a few words for my uncle's funeral, which I read to the parishioners. It was a very moving piece, which caused a great many tears.

The hardest thing was at the gravesite for the family gathered around the casket for their final farewell. Poor Mom almost passed out. She had to be helped up for her legs could no longer carry her. We then went to the wake and gathered our wits and had something to eat. Everyone showed up, even two uncles from Calgary.

I spent a few more days at my aunt's apartment before returning to Victoria. That was the final chapter to my relationship with a dear man who raised me as his own son. I have the deepest respect and love for this man, and I am proud to call him, "Dad."

My biological father stayed a smoker and drinker till his own demise. In the past few years, I would visit him almost every day when I was in town. Apparently, this gave him great pleasure to have a few drinks with his own son. For all the troubles in the past, he believed that I forgave him. However, the hurt was still there. I loved him, but only to a certain point. I did have my boundaries with him.

This was not the end of my concerns. Within two years, my biological father fell ill. He had trouble breathing which was not surprising for he smoked two packs of cigarettes a day for fifty years. He also was weak and sleeping a lot. Christmas was only a week or so away, and he was invited to come for dinner at my Auntie Katie's house.

My dad was too ill to attend. Soon after, he stopped smoking. My stepsister told me of his condition, and they were going to put him in hospital. She said that he was ill and that she would keep in touch with me if there were any changes.

A few times she called, and sometimes he grew worse while other times, he improved. It didn't seem like anything to panic about. The following Tuesday, he was dead. Just like that; it was over.

The following day, I was in Winnipeg and my stepsister had everything under control as far as the funeral was concerned. My other stepsister from Ontario caught the plane later that night.

The funeral was a few days later. It was an open-casket ceremony. I didn't shed one single tear for him. Deep inside, I was still angry with him for putting me in a foster home where I was sexually assaulted. I had so much I wanted to tell him, and now he was gone.

It was not until several months after the funeral that my stepsister revealed the truth about my father. He did not want me to leave home. He was forced by social services to volunteer custody to the province, or they would come in the middle of the night and take me. It was revealed that my biological mother also suffered from hypersexual tendencies. However, she couldn't refrain from taking on those actions. Within a year, they were divorced.

I have been born and raised among farmers. Booze has always been a family staple. Even my severely depressed mother hit the juice pretty hard from time to time. My entire life seems to revolve around this woman. This is a woman that I really do not know. She was apparently diagnosed with manic depression some time back. She never told me anything about it. Then again, that would have been a very difficult thing for her to do. My birth mother and I have never spent more than thirty days together in nearly forty years of life.

In honesty, I do not have any real love for her. I cannot love a person if a personal bond has not been established. It seems that she has a real love for me, but I am unable to feel any real love for her.

How can I love this woman? I have a hard time getting over

her mental disabilities. When I see her, all I see is a severely ill woman. This could not be my mother.

Her bond for me is much stronger than what I have for her. The first two weeks that we were together didn't mean a damn thing to me. I was only two weeks old. She was very ill at that time and life became unbearable for my biological father. Her behaviours were unpredictable, so my father packed up and left, taking me with him. He did this for he was not sure if I would be safe being alone with her.

I do not remember anything because of my age. Is it wrong that I honestly do not love her? Many members of the family are very surprised that I don't have an unconditional love for this woman. I have more love for a dearly departed goldfish that I had when I was only six years old than for my own mother. I did not see her again until I was twelve years old; I knew my gold fish for almost two years. My biological mother's mental illness was having havoc on her at this time. Behaviour problems and drinking clouded her head of any thoughts of me. She lived on the system as a pauper and stayed in her closet for many years.

It may be possible that this is a connection that I must make in order for me to heal. In reality, I have no will to ever see her again. Another sad thing is that I really don't want to see anyone from my own family again. The amount of time apart from them has buried any affection that I once really treasured.

In honesty, I have no love for anyone that has truly loved me. Many years ago, the love that was in my heart died. I really do not feel any love for anyone, not even for myself.

This was about the time I went into a two-year bed ridden depression. All I did was sleep and drink booze. I didn't eat or sleep properly, and I gained sixty-five pounds of fat around my waist. I had no energy left in my body to do anything. I had no goals or ambitions for the future; I was just rotting between the bed sheets.

Of course, this depression was drug-induced. I would remain

this way for as long as I was drinking. The one good thing about the depression was that I was not suffering from any manias or psychosis. The depression kept my mood low enough to stop these occurrences from happening. In a way, this was a very good thing. At least I was safe at home and not gallivanting up and down the darkened streets.

This depression could have been triggered by my uncle's and Dad's deaths; I'm not sure. I know that they were very close, and they meant a great deal to me. There wasn't a day pass me by that I didn't think of them. Maybe, this was my way of grieving. I didn't think I was affected by my uncle's death, for I knew he was in a better place. I felt that we said our piece to each other and were content with our efforts. I felt a sense of relief when he passed on for he was no longer suffering. It was sad to see him during the last two days of his life. He was in very bad shape.

Whatever the reason for the depression, it took a mania to snap me out of it. This was when I decided to write a four hundred-page novel. I was wild with enthusiasm. Without any thought or planning, I just started too free-write. The ideas were just there, snowballing on top of each other.

I didn't have to think. Everything was falling into place. However, because of the recent depression I had suffered, there was a definite dark tone to the book. The darkness in my soul found its way onto the pages of the manuscript. This did scare people. Some were scared of me for I was the one who wrote it, while others loved it.

What was to be a crime/drama soon took on a life of its own. My own experiences with mental illness and addiction were being carefully intertwined with the story, which gave it a bizarre twist. If you read between the lines, it is a story of my life through a fictional character.

I couldn't write fast enough for the ideas were jumping onto the paper. This lasted nine months wherein I finished the novel. Then it took about six months to edit it. By that time, I was already in another depression. I found the editing very difficult for my mind was obscured by illness. I must have re-read the manuscript thirty times before sending it off to the printers. Even so, there are still mistakes in it.

The book was written cover-to-cover without revisions or editing; only spelling errors were corrected. The book is raw, and it would not do it justice if it were done any other way. My interpretation of life is much darker than the general public's. This was what I wanted to portray in the book. Mental illness and addiction is a rough road to travel, and I wanted people to understand this.

This was my introduction about mental illness and addiction for the public. Through an entertaining story, they would be also taught about the different affects of these conditions. It was almost like reading a textbook, for the details and explanations were there.

Patrick J. Schnerch

Nowhere to hide

As I reflect back, Uncle Adam's drinking had a profound affect on me, and now I realize how serious it really was. I was literally hiding from him because I was scared of him. This fear almost lasted my entire lifetime. Only now do I understand him and where he was coming from. He was not very sociable when he was drinking. Perhaps, he wasn't there for me when I needed his love the most. I dismissed him as a reliable source of love and affection and held on tight to my Auntie Jessie who gave me love and protection.

Perhaps, then I was consumed by darkness; I was looking for an escape, even if it meant my own death. At first, my mind shut down blocking the terrible past from haunting me, and then I was looking for something more permanent. This started a life of despair and uncertainty. Together with the isolation and culture shock I was bound to become a victim.

The damage was done. Hanging on to the apron strings of my aunt and the morals implanted in my soul, I had nowhere else to turn but inward. I couldn't rely on my uncle for protection or guidance during those formative years. I needed a male figure in my life, and he wasn't there. I needed his strength and wisdom to prepare me for life in the real world, not the sheltered settings of home.

I never realized the damage caused from what I thought was a happy childhood. Alcohol was my enemy from a very early age and has plagued me all my life. My happy thoughts and memories of my youth are now tarnished by this realization. The seed was implanted very early in my life; it just was a matter of time before it would manifest itself into a problem. The suicidal thoughts still continue, turning all harm inwards.

Alcohol not only caused problems for my uncle, but it also affected the whole family, including me. I didn't think that his drinking would have such a strong influence on me more than four decades later, but it did.

Not only did I grow up surrounded by alcohol, even at birth, it was in my blood. Both my biological mother and father were alcoholics at that time. My father continued until his very own death. There is no escaping this deadly elixir. It has swallowed me whole.

It seems to be of no wonder why I wanted to die when I was eight years old. I was already scarred. This seems to be the most reasonable explanation for a young boy thinking that there was nothing left. This has followed me throughout my life and into my own alcoholism. I was so happy during my childhood that I blocked out the pain from my memory. The darkness kept me safe.

Depression can be extremely overwhelming and dangerous. It attacks your mind and soul. Without your defences in place, you are in the grips of fate. You do not have your thoughts of family, loved ones, or friends that would be hurt if you were gone. There is nothing holding you back from the inevitable.

It is emotions that drive the body into action. If you are feeling emotional pain, there is no thought process when dragging a sharp blade up your forearm or wrists. All you feel is hurt and despair. There is no life in your heart, only darkness.

I have suffered literally hundreds of depressive episodes. Some were relatively calm, while others landed me in hospital. With my soul blackened, there is nothing left. My loved ones will get over the shock of my absence in their own time. There is no self-esteem, pride, or will to survive. I have already died a thousand deaths.

I have been fighting it. Every day I try something new to help lift my spirits. Failures in my home life, employment, finances, and social aspects of my life keep me down. My biggest failure was to my wife and her family. I have let her down. I am unable to be the man she deserves. I tried to get another job, but I cracked within two weeks. I tried running the household and repairs and was overwhelmed. Worst of all, I tried to be a husband, but I crashed and burned.

It was not known until a psychotic episode that writing would become a passion of mine. I had a compulsion to write The Third Testament for I believed I was God's messenger. I did write it, and I blasted humanity for the evils that we are faced with today.

I couldn't stop writing. There was so much to say. I would work all day and night and into the early morning hours. I was deprived of sleep and nutrition. There was a deadline, which had to be kept as dictated by God. This lasted several months while I was in a mania. The psychosis caused the ramblings and the thoughts of a spiritual nature.

It was during that time that I first documented parts of my life to paper. An overview was the general idea. I dealt with my on-going experiences with mental illness and the problematic behaviour that was developing at that time.

A new doctor arrived on the scene, and he looked at the writings. He came to the conclusion that I was in a psychotic state. He prescribed new medication and the writings immediately stopped. Even the problematic behaviour was arrested by this new medication and so that was the end of my psychosis.

I was later shocked at the contents of the book. I asked a friend to read it, and she was amazed. Even though I was very ill at the time, the writing itself was pretty good. This was the very first time that I have ever written anything, and I seemed to have a natural flair for it. It's true that I was totally out of my head, but there was also something there.

I never finished high school or went to college, and I didn't understand my English studies. However, my writings had a distinctive style. I don't know where it came from, but it seemed that I might have stumbled across something. This seemed to be where my heart was; my emotions and soul came alive on paper. I could never speak that well, but I can convey it through my writings.

The wild random thoughts of that manuscript inspired me to continue in my writings. At some point, I started journaling as well. Then during another mania, I wrote a three hundred ninety-seven-page crime/drama. The story intertwined with a life living with mental illness and addiction. Although fictional with the crime plot, some segments regarding alcoholism and mental illness were quite accurate. The psychotic memories from the recent past were still fresh in my mind when I wrote that book. Many people thought that it was too dark and scary. I hate sugar wrapping a story. If I want you to know something, I am going to damn well say it. It left a bad taste in their mouths, but I felt that artistically it had to be told that way.

After that I fell into a two-year drug induced depression. My days consisted of drinking all day and sleeping all night. I didn't know what day it was or if I ever had a wife. I never saw her during that time because I was passed out before she came home from work. That was the time that I gave up on myself.

My failures had overcome me, and I could no longer face them. I didn't care what people thought of me anymore. There was no pride or a will to take my next breath. I didn't want to live anymore. I was too tired. By this time there had been tests done on my liver, which showed that there was damage on the outer edges. The hardening of the liver was caused by my drinking habits. I was rotting from the inside, out. I was drinking almost forty ounces of rye a day plus two litres of soda. Something had to be done. I had one foot in the grave and the other on a banana peel.

I went to an addictions clinic for help. There was a combination of one-to-one counselling and support groups. I managed to stop drinking for about six weeks or so. This continued for two years at the clinic. My record was poor and my counsellor decided that I should go through detox, which a seven day is drying out period is monitored by nurses.

An amazing transformation happened when I walked through those doors. I made the decision to give up alcohol and take back control of my life. I felt this heavy burden lift from my shoulders. I had made a commitment to myself to stop the booze and move on in life. All of the sudden, I saw the world through a different light. I felt emotions and feelings again. I came alive once again. I never felt that way for over thirty years and finally everything opened up to me. I had choices that I never had before.

My heart and soul came alive. I had ambitions and goals for a bright future. It was wonderful to be alive. I was writing a manuscript, which included all my journals and writings under one cover. It also included the manuscript written while in psychosis. The book covered my life while being affected by different conditions such as psychosis, depression, mania, alcoholism, treatment, and recovery.

This manuscript shed light on mental illness and addiction. It was an inside look at these conditions for they were written while being captured in those particular moments. Suicidal thoughts were documented as they were happening. Manias and insanity were frozen in time as they hit the paper. It was a very enlightening experience as I was reliving my past. Pieces were falling into place, creating a whole new picture of what had already transpired.

It was challenging work for I was revealing all my secrets to the public. I bore all in this work, not leaving a single stone unturned. I believed that the truth had to be out in the open. Using myself as a sacrificial lamb, it became obsessive to tell everyone of what it was like to live in hell on earth.

Not understanding the audience that would read this book, I continued writing in a daze. Tragic memories and experiences haunted my soul for decades looking for a release. I finally found my reason for being. I was to tell others my particular story for their own enlightenment so they can learn and understand these conditions that affect millions of people worldwide.

I am only one person with a story that I believe must be told. Educating and informing others that we are survivors who have overcome great obstacles may help others to learn and understand, thus removing stigma and prejudice.

During this sober period, I started my own business and newsletter, which is distributed throughout the city and on the web. This breath of fresh air gave me my life back. I was productive and on a mission. I felt this connection with the less fortunate, and I wanted to help. I do this by the newsletter. I give useful information, hope, and inspiration for a brighter tomorrow.

Mental illness is unforgiving for it affects all walks of life. The less fortunate are prime examples, for many of them are unable to work for a living. Either they live off the system or on the streets. Many do not have hope for a happy future. They struggle daily just to survive. I have a deep compassion for these people for they need support and understanding from the public.

There are agencies and organizations designed to help their needs, but many of those places are overwhelmed by the demand. They are also struggling with support or donations to keep their clients in a state of well-being. Many of these places also have large caseloads and waiting lists for services. Time is not a commodity for these people. They need help now.

This is my mission, to relay where these services are and what is available. I tell people how to contact these organizations and what programs are available. I act as a liaison officer between the street and society at large. They are my friends, and I care for them. They deserve better lives, for they are forced by circumstance to fight for survival. Many cannot handle the conditions and turn to addictions to numb the pain. At least if they don't feel the torture, it makes it easier to wake up the next morning.

No one deserves an existence such as that. I don't care who you are or what you do. That is not acceptable. Society turns a blind eye to these people. As long as they are not in your backyard, you really don't give a damn if they live or die. That line of thinking has to change.

They are real people, too. They have needs that are not being met. It could happen so easy to anyone; you don't understand how lucky we are. We can lose our jobs or have a divorce and we can find ourselves on the street. Highly depressed with your situation, you turn to alcohol to relieve the hurt. Soon, you are addicted and become part of the system. It happens every day; it's just that easy.

What would happen if you were hit by illness? Your life would be changed forever. Think of people with schizophrenia or manic depression. Their life falls apart after their diagnosis. Their family and friends, in many cases, abandon them, leaving them to fend for themselves, alone and desperate. This is very real and frightening.

Thank your stars that you have a roof over your head and food in your stomach. Hundreds of people are homeless in this small city and thousands are on disability benefits in this province. It's not much, but at least they are out of the cold. Mental illness is a killer of the mind, body, and soul.

This has become my goal in life: to help others, like me, to get their chance at a better future. My life was basically perfect compared to some of the stories I heard from others. Their lives are full of tragedy and despair with troubles compounding daily. Some have used intravenous drugs, and now they have hepatitis or HIV. If they didn't get it from the drugs, some prostituted themselves to get their fix and got a disease from sexual transmission.

Living on the streets is also becoming very violent. Stabbings, shootings, and beatings are almost a daily occurrence. These unfortunate people live in the heart of this violence. Some homes are violent, hostile environments, where children cannot grow up to be healthy productive adults because they are surrounded by drugs and booze. A large percentage of people with addiction problems are also mentally ill, though not yet diagnosed. It is very difficult to diagnose a mental illness while addicted. They are numbed by their drugs, which keep the symptoms of the illness at bay. Without being in tune with your body, an illness is rarely detected. I went through most of my life under the influence of alcohol; as a result, the illness did not affect me as much as it might have. Having another drink covered the problem. When the numbness wore off, and I was feeling bad again, there was always the bottle to soothe my soul.

It was a coping strategy that worked for many years; however, it didn't help the fight against the psychosis. I was still out of control. Some people do not believe in doctors and medication and cope solely on their addictions to get them through. As long as they stay out of the hospital, this is something that works to a certain degree. However, many other problems arise from addiction.

There are mental, physical, financial, and social aspects that are controlled by the addiction. Even without illness, you are no longer in control of your life. Your addiction does that for you. To get in touch with the real you, the addiction must stop before your life can be evaluated at face value. As difficult as it seems, this is the only way to salvation. These are the facts; the addiction must stop.

We have to look deep into our hearts, and we will find the real truth. Addiction is not the answer; it only masks the problem. Of course, this is easier said than done. This could be the most difficult decision you ever have to make. You have to see your reflection in the mirror and make a choice. Do you want a better life or don't you? The ball is in your court; you have to decide what you are going to do about it.

I am facing my demons right now. I have to make that deciding choice of what I am going to do next. Do I want to continue with my dreams and goals or am I going to sink to the depths of hell. At this present time, hell doesn't look that bad. I don't really know what I should do.

I want stories from the destitute. I want to interview prostitutes and get their stories of what is the driving force behind their actions. Are they ill or addicted? I want to know the answers to my many questions. Do they really enjoy having sex with a total stranger? How do they get in the mood for a less than desirable customer? Is money the object of this game? Do they have any morals left or has morality been dismissed from their troubled past? Is it drugs that help them sleep at night so that they can wake up to a new day? There has to be reasons behind their suffering. I am determined to find out the truth.

There are stories out there that need to be told. The soup kitchens are loaded with people who are hungry and in need of something to eat. The emergency shelters are full of people needing to rest their weary head for a night's sleep. Clothing, housing, medical and dental treatment are essential parts of life. There are places that provide these services free of charge or at minimal cost. These places are great for emergency services to the destitute. However, with a little will power, they can become productive members of society again and live stable lives under a roof with food in their stomach.

The main way to recovery is to drop the addiction. This also includes cigarettes for it is a financial burden that eats up the money needed for survival such as food and shelter. With limited income, priorities have to be adhered to. Personal gratification must be the least of your concerns. Survival must come first.

I have a great concern for all of these people, and I want them to be happy about themselves and their future. I want to help them change their lives and become survivors. There are many personal choices that have to be made before any changes happen. The newsletter is useful in outlining the choices available.

This has become my mission in life as well as the other publications that my company supports. I wrote some while others are contributions of other authors. As a writing family, our thoughts and dreams are written on paper and shared with the world.

What about my future? I have to now educate myself for my future as a writer. I have the stories and the passion, but I don't have the skill to put it together as an exciting novel. I lack in education. I need to learn how to set-up a plot and keep the suspense moving at a quick pace. My skill in introducing characters and building their personalities needs polishing.

I am already capable of writing an interesting novel, but I need to know how to write a great book. I want the people to be captured by my stories and bound by the grips of suspense. My audience and their satisfaction mean a great deal to me. I want them to have a high quality product.

Although my writing is important, I'm not sure if it will be successful. Most authors are university-trained students with degrees in writing. I have to compete with people who are highly skilled in their trade. Although I have something they don't have. That's an original story.

My storyline is original and very different. It's so different that people have to take a second look at it to confirm their understanding. It has a bizarre twist to the story. It certainly isn't a straightforward book. There is a story behind the story. Most people like the book, some love it, and a couple of people couldn't read it. This last work was my humble beginning. I could scratch "ADRIAN" off as a learning experience.

It is a patient's point of view, distorted or not. There are a lot of books out there on manic depression written by doctors, but the patients themselves write few. It is the front line look at the illness through the eyes of the victim. The thoughts and feelings are captured on paper as they happen. The pain and anguish are real.

The patient really doesn't know what is real or not. Their perspective could be inadvertently distorted. What they feel can be just the manner in which they look at things. If their thinking were negative, their whole outlook on life would be grim. Even if things are actually on the upside, they have a hard time finding the good in it.

When in a manic high, their whole life is full of high spirits and euphoria. They will spend truckloads of money that they don't have. They will party all night, every night.

The energy shoots out of their bodies. Nothing could go wrong. Reality is not a factor. Overdue bills, collection agencies, and sheriff visits are downplayed. Reckless behaviour and sexual advances are the norm. Being brought home by the police or spending the night in jail is also frequent behaviour.

Those are not our realities, but that is the world we live in. The truths are distorted and exaggerated or downplayed at times. When reality does return, then the pain and torment really begin. The truths usually never reach us. Only now, after so many years, have I come to realize some of those truths. It will still take time to discover the other realities that were hidden in my world.

Healing from such profound disturbances may take years before they come to the surface. Lately, some discoveries were unveiled for me, revealing secrets of a distorted past. Bits and pieces eventually fall into place and show the big picture.

Most mentally ill people don't achieve this satisfaction. Their minds are clouded with illusions. On Christmas Day, I believed that the police were after me even though they weren't. I truly believed they were following me. It scared the crap out of me. My fears were real, but the situation was distorted. My truth was an illusion of my mind.

I believed I was ready to work again. The realities were then later revealed and disappointment set in. This was another illusion that blinded me from the truth. I must be capable of something, but I spent my whole life looking for it without success. I'm getting older, and I am not satisfied with my situation. Time is passing me by.

These are some of the realities that I am capable of comprehending. Some of these truths are very hurtful. It is hard to feel good about yourself when success in life passes you by. It has been a constant battle trying to succeed at something. I have no direction. I don't know where to start.

I have taken inventory of my life. I did have limited success with some of my ventures. I even accomplished something quite amazing. It just doesn't seem to be enough. I could very well be a perfectionist who believes it is all or nothing. I have to realize that nothing is perfect. There is always room for improvement. I think this is the new me.

I have become more realistic. I try not to let my illness get in the way of my thinking, although these swirling random thoughts are impulsive. These thoughts are processed in milliseconds, and there is very little time to rationalize those images. It is very easy to get swept away into a fantasy. Things are not always as they appear; you see what you want to see. This is the world of manic depression.

Homecoming

There were some things in my life that changed me forever. Some of those things were traumatic and damaging to the point that I never did recover, even to this day. The two most traumatic times were the move to my biological father's house and the other was the sexual assault.

I never did get over those events. My doctor now insists that I am more content feeling miserable, a habit that manifested itself at an early stage in my life. He also believes that my problem is alcohol-induced. I disagree with him. Drinking or not, I have still gone through depressive and mania episodes.

Even my editor believes that something horrific happened in my first five years of life. He wanted me to elaborate on my early years in an attempt to reveal the cause. I find this very difficult, for I only remember happy times during that period. The one thing that did harm me was the isolation. I also remember being quite timid around other children when they came to visit, even if they were cousins of mine.

When they came over, I felt intimidated by their presence. Apparently, my biological father also had that problem when he was a child. When guests came to his house, he used to run and hide under the bed and cry until they left. I wasn't quite as bad, but the feelings were the same. I felt more comfortable with my mom and dad without any guests. I was scared of people in general. I often had a hard time getting along with other children. Encounters with them usually escalated into confrontations. I was also very insecure, just like my biological father.

However, I think that my relationship with my uncle was severely damaged by his alcoholism. I relied on my aunt as the only parent. My mild manners and timid behaviour stem from her. I resented my uncle for what he was doing, and I kept away from his path. I think this had further repercussions later in my life. I spent my early childhood afraid and uncertain about life.

Every time an uncle would come over, out would come a couple bottles of rye. A couple of my uncles would not go home until the booze dried up. My dad had to sometimes stash a bottle out of sight before they came over or they would have drunk everything.

The mania is not as prominent now as before. I just get overly happy and excited now. I spend more money than I have and have little care for the immediate future. It becomes a big party for a few months. This becomes a real problem because where there is a party--there is always booze. I spend large amounts of money in the bar every month. I could easily spend sixteen hundred dollars in a month.

A hundred dollars a day in the pub kept me entertained from mid-day till closing time. Do this every day, and it adds up fast. My wife and I had to come to an agreement that I relinquish my credit card and ATM card over to her. I am unable to manage finances as I once did before. I can drink vast amounts of alcohol that would put most serious drunks under the table.

Until I go back into rehabilitation, my wife and I agreed that I could drink at home under certain conditions. I must take my empties back and try to moderate my habits so that a case a beer will last for a while. Conservation for an alcoholic like me is like giving a horse a tablespoon of water and think that its thirst is quenched. I try to slow down, but I still have urges in the morning, which are pretty hard to resist.

I normally wake up around 3:00 A.M. and drink a couple of pots of coffee. After that, I am wound right up and need something to relax me. So I drink three beers to calm me down. This yo-yo affect lasts all day until I go to bed at night. When I get jittery, I wash it down with a beer. Sometimes I will take short naps during the day to sleep off the effects of the alcohol. Feeling refreshed after a nap, I'll grab another beer. Before you know it, by evening I have already drunk a dozen beers.

It is no wonder my liver is as hard as a stone. For some reason,

I have a character of doing things all the way or not at all. There is no in between for me. This is also true with my addictions. Whatever I do, there is no happy medium. This goes for work, play, smoking, and drinking. I'm a big lump of preventable disease, and I don't care. I could lessen the chances of becoming ill if I would only take care of myself. I just don't want to.

When I was intimate with my wife, I didn't make love to her, I raped her. Everything I do is over the edge. I have no self-control. This is especially true when I am in a bar or walking the streets. Whatever the mood I am in will dictate what will happen next. It is not a thought-out plan but an impulse to the situation.

Being mentally ill and fuelled by alcohol makes me an unpredictable and dangerous man. I don't think with my head; I think with my emotions. I will go through great lengths to fulfill my desires whether it is sexual or homicidal. There are no rules, regulations or consequences that will stop me from my quest. People are only targets or things; they have no value in my world.

Nothing matters in this state of mind. My home life and the consequence of losing it all do not calculate in my mind. I am free to do as I wish and when I wish. I am cold, emotionless, and dark when in my world. You can count your lucky stars that you are alive when in my presence. Feelings and emotions are downplayed. Begging is shunned. This is my playground now!

The only way to stop me is to kill me and you can bet your bottom dollar that I am going to take you with me. Together, we will both burn in hell. Do or die. That is my motto. To die is an honour if you have a cause. There is always a reason for living or dying.

My reason for living is to help the less fortunate to feel the wonders of life before they die. They must feel the goodness of really living. Whether it is raising a child or content in a loving relationship, this is real life. Being wanted and needed is a great gift. Everyone should experience some form of happiness in his or her life, even if it is only briefly.

When there is no longer happiness in your life and you have exhausted all your resources, then it's time to die. I've been dead inside for many years and now I am waiting for my body to catch up. I have no respect for myself anymore. I have given up hope of ever being happy again. I'm not saying that this is a bad thing; everyone is going to die. I just prefer sooner than later.

One of the most critical factors in my feeling this way is the fact that we do not have children. Without children, your life is almost meaningless. I will never go full circle. There was no child bonding, graduation, marriages, or grandchildren. There are no Christmas dinners or birthday parties with the family, no Sunday night dinners at grandma's house. Our lives are empty. I already lived my life; there is nothing left. I truly envy people with children—their lives are complete.

In a way, this is a blessing in disguise. At least, I won't be passing this dreaded illness to my children. That's what happened to me. It was passed on from my mother. There is a fifty/fifty chance of passing the illness to my children. That is a very high risk in ruining someone's life.

It was later admitted to me that my birth mother has manic depression. She showed me her blister pack of familiar anti-depressants. She had a very rough time growing up in an age where little was known about mental illness. Back then; they blamed my father for her condition because of his work schedule.

They gave her medication that damaged her eyesight and many rounds of electric shock therapy.

Nothing worked. She was out of control. She was at one time an alcoholic, during the same period as her illness. There was hypersexual activity that finally led to divorce. She was extremely ill in those days.

Today, she is on disability pension living on her own. Her meagre survival seems to be all she needs. She is happy and content with her life and her medication is working out just fine. It is much less than a glamorous existence, but she is managing.

When I see her, I see a mirror image of myself. We look the same; we have the same hair and face, not to mention the same illness. I look nothing like my father. He was tall, dark, and built like a brick shit house. I think I also have her kind heart. My father was a stubborn man and would not listen to reason.

After forty-five years of existence, that is all I know about my birth parents. Our relationship was largely spanned over time interrupted by short visits. Years would pass without seeing each other, and no one cared.

When I lived with my biological father, he never told me that I was ill. I found out many years later on my own. If I knew, that would have explained all the trouble I was having, especially with my behaviour. He never told me why I was going to a foster home. I just believed he didn't want me anymore. Two weeks after arriving at the home, I was sexually assaulted. For over thirty years I blamed my father for that assault for he was the one who put me there. I carried this anger for over three decades. When he died, and I saw his face in the casket, all those memories resurfaced bringing me pain and anguish.

Several months later, my stepsister told me what really happened. Now, I feel guilty that I carried this hatred for all these years. He should have talked to me, but he didn't and it caused a lot of grief. Now, it's too late to say 'I'm sorry,' or 'I love you Dad.' He is gone and he took all his secrets with him. There were many more secrets I wasn't told, secrets that I am slowly discovering only now. It just didn't have to be that way.

It seems that my medication is working most of the time. I could go through most of the year unaffected by illness. That's the way it should be anyway. The only problem is sometimes a depression will overcome the medication and render the drugs useless. Last year, I wasn't drinking during my last depression, and I was close to losing my mind and life. I never did resort to the bottle, but it was hell on earth. My doctor blames the alcohol for the depression. He figures that I am sabotaging his treatment by drinking.

He is extremely angry with me, and I believe he has lost his grip. I went nearly my entire life with illness and many years went by without addiction, but I was still screwed up. He believes that I enjoy misery. I would like to stick his chair up his ass and see if he is not traumatized by the event. I'm quite certain that he would not be a happy camper. Why is it any different for me? Pulled away from loving parents and put into turmoil also had implications. Over thirty years of illness, several doctors have confirmed that I suffer from bi-polar disorder. I have a mother who is barely surviving from this illness, and I am told that I enjoy it.

I don't enjoy it! It is all I know. I don't feel happiness. I don't know what it feels like. I am damaged goods, and I am not getting any help from him. It is true that I also suffer from a character defect; there is no denying that. Those two events did cause damage. That is, however, not the whole story. If it was, why didn't he cure me by now?

The drinking is the only happiness I know that works. If the doctor cured the problem, I would no longer have a reason to drink. That is the only time I feel good about life. In my own world, nothing goes wrong. Everything is happy and secure. When I enter your world, life collapses.

The darkness is where I belong. This is a place where I am welcome. I disassociate from the living and join the dead. Maybe, I can see things that no one else sees. There is a whole different dimension out there. Don't be afraid of the dark!

My body is still pumping blood, but I am already dead. It's not as bad as you may think. It's peaceful, free from turmoil. I have an open communication with my dearly departed. My grandma and grandpa welcome me with open arms. My Uncle Adam says, "You don't belong here." My Uncle Joe agrees. My biological father is thrilled about our relationship. My Uncle Johnny was very depressed, and I told him that he was ill. It is an open door. I communicate all the time, but I have to disassociate from reality to do it. Most of the time, I can open the gates to darkness by drinking; other times I can do it without my addiction.

Most people seek happiness, and I am no different. I just find my joy on the other side. I have nothing on this earth. In the darkness, I have love, passion, and desire. It is no mystery why I am addicted. I want to live, but not here.

This is why my life on earth has no meaning; there is much more out there than you can ever imagine. There most certainly is life after death. I've been there, done that! It's wonderful! There is no pain or anguish; all is peaceful. The darkness is where it's at. That is why I have no fear of death. In fact, I welcome it with open arms.

There is nothing to be afraid of. Tranquility is a precious commodity, which is very hard to achieve on this earth. Out there, it is abundant. I feel so good and comfortable in the darkness that trying to stop my passage is unthinkable. Yet, that is what I am supposed to do. I am supposed to live my life here in pain and anguish. I can still disassociate without alcohol, but it is a little bit harder to achieve. All I need is one beer to relax me enough to put me in my comfortable place.

It sounds like bullshit—I realize that. I really believe, however, that it is my psychosis returning, or I am absolutely mad. Maybe, I am losing my connection with reality and I am hallucinating. I don't know. All I know is that it feels very real to me. I love my place, whether it is real or not.

I honestly believe that I can project my soul to my own world. For some reason, it is easier to accomplish with the aid of alcohol. While in my world, there are interruptions from reality. I can participate in your world, but my mind and soul are consumed by the darkness. It the intrusions of the outside reality that feel like rude interruptions from the place where I feel happy and content with myself when I drink. Perhaps, it is nothing more than the drug talking. I just know I feel immeasurable pleasure in the darkness. I don't like the consequences of my actions, and I know I have to change. To give up my quiet place for a stable life on earth is not very inviting.

I have to give up my happiness and live a life of disgust, because I'm not acceptable otherwise. That is when the suicidal thoughts come back. I need to go back to my happy place. I will get there one way or another.

I am to live the rest of my year's miserable and suicidal gathering scar tissue all over my body. No one has ever shown me one fuck'n thing to be happy about. Granted, I had some laughs, but seldom and very far apart. I howl when I'm on the other side. It is simple euphoria within the shades of black. There I belong.

It sounds ridiculous. I understand that. This is my belief, however, not yours. I have earned my right to believe in my own hallucinations and myself. Real or not, they are mine! When I die, I will be a very happy man.

There is a place on earth where I do belong and that is on the streets. It, too, is a separate world from the rest of society. It is a lonely existence. I feel welcome on the streets by the inhabitants. In my work, I see hundreds of people in need. There are hundreds of reasons why they are out there, and they are mostly all valid. Some are mentally ill while many are addicted. Unable to work, they take flight to the streets. There is no other place to go.

It could happen to me very easily if I continue the path I'm on. My wife in near giving up hope for me, and she is now contemplating her next move. My aunt is disappointed with me, and my doctor is furious. I haven't got a friend in the world except my drinking buddy. Even he thinks I need to quit. I know that the drinking is destroying me and is one of the leading causes of my distress, but I'm not ready yet.

I was ready last time. I felt it in my soul. Stopping drinking was fairly easy because I was mentally ready for it. This time, the drinking is doing me a tremendous favour by keeping me stable. I'm still pretty shaky, but I am managing. My doctor told me that I'm on a large dose of medication, which he cannot increase while I am drinking.

That's fine. I'm surviving and coping quite well. Unfortunately, other people don't see it that way. They are not liars; they tell me what they see. They see me wasting my life away, and it hurts them to see me that way. This is especially true for my wife. She sees the real me while I don't. I am in my own little world, unaware of the hurt that I am causing.

When I quit last time, I realized what I had done to everyone. Now I am oblivious as to what I am doing. Financing my habits is the most difficult thing to do right now, and yet I am not concerned of what I am doing. I will drain our account to fill my habit. I already did that once.

Today, I understand what I am doing. Perhaps, thinking about the situation will slowly ready me for rehabilitation. I am causing too much grief for my family. Something has to change because I am dragging other people down with me. It seems that I am unable to have it both ways. When I drink, I drink a lot. I can't seem to stop after only a few. If it only were a few beers, I would be all right. I drink all day, however, which is where the problem lies.

It just does not justify me drinking all the time. The peace of mind and tranquility when drinking is overwhelming. The dark place is so soothing to the soul and that it is very difficult to escape from. The enormous pleasures override any thoughts of reality.

Not knowing if this is part of the illness or the addiction, the power it has over me is tremendous. There is no depression present. There hasn't been any for a very long time. Depression should be present if an addiction is involved.

The alcohol is a depressant, and when consumed, it produces a drug-induced depression. This works to your favour if you are in a mania. If you are depressed already, then you are about to have a rough ride. However, right now I'm in a happy medium even with the alcohol.

The only thing that affects my work is the alcohol. Even one can of beer impairs me enough not to think clearly and make mistakes. I have to realize that my work is more important than alcohol. Actually, my whole life is more important than alcohol. Even though I know this, I still don't do what I preach. It seems that the booze has taken over my life and that it is more important than anything else in the world.

It is the inner peace that I have grown accustomed to. My mind shuts off, blocking out reality. There is no sadness or sorrow in my world. All is tranquil. This state of mind, however, causes me to be useless in real life.

I loose touch with everything that is real. The imaginations that take hold of my soul bring me happiness and contentment.

I see darkness all around me; from the corner of my eye, I can see my dearly departed Uncle Adam. He, the couch, the coffee table, and the TV, which is on the Family Channel, are illuminated. Unaware of my presence, he hovers over the coffee table eating his sunflower seeds. There is a ring of empty shells surrounding his feet on the floor.

I approach him with a smile and open arms. My uncle gets up and gives me a big hug. He said, "You're not supposed to be here." I said, "I know, Dad, but I have to." I ask, "Dad, do you want a hot chocolate?" He answered, "Yes, please." I move into the darkness and retrieve two hot chocolates. I put them on the table and sit down beside my dad.

I say, "Mom really misses you a lot. She had a real hard time getting used to being alone. She thought that you were too young to go." Dad said, "It was my time. Not like you. You have so much to live for and you spend your life here in the darkness. I belong here. I love you and we will keep in touch, but you have a house, wife, and dog to take care of. Don't waste your life at the bottom of a whiskey bottle. Be a man and take charge. You have everything going for you. I lived a good long life. I had my troubles, too, but I got over them. So can you."

I said, "I know Dad, it just seems like there is nothing left for me over there. At least here, I have you. It's so peaceful here. You and I connect. Even when I phoned you and told you that I would be home for Christmas, we both knew that you were going to die. You knew why I was coming home. I wanted to see you one last time before it were too late. You waited for the family to see you on Christmas Day to say your final good-byes. Then, December 26th, 2000, you quietly passed away in your sleep. Mom was devastated. I was deeply saddened, but happy for you for you are now in a better place."

Dad said, "I'm so happy you came. We had a real nice talk before I got too sick. I got to say my piece to you face to face. That was one of the highlights of my life. Even though it was so near to the end, I still felt happiness and joy." I said, "I know Dad, I felt the same way. I will treasure that moment in my heart for an eternity. It really made a difference in my life to hear those words come from you. I have always had a lot of respect for you. Your words are etched in stone deep into my very soul."

Dad said, "Now, I think it is time for you to go back and show Kathy that you love her. You can do much better than you have been. You have given up on yourself. It is time to pick yourself up off the floor and dust yourself off. Don't feel sorry for yourself. Do something; you have it inside of you. You have a good life going for you; don't waste it. Remember that I will be watching you. Now go back and treat her right."

I got up from the couch and walked towards the darkness. My dad followed close behind. With tears in my eyes, I turned around and gave him a big hug and told him that I loved him. He said, "I love you too, go home…"

This vision is so real to me that it had a dramatic affect on my behaviour. It helped ground me to the real world and with my wife. I have neglected her for years, causing her to fend by herself. I feel ashamed and not worthy of her love, but she is always there for me.

I also have my dog Blackie. We had him since he was six weeks old. He was on demand feeding and we used to give him water with an eyedropper. Blackie was so tiny that he fit into the palm of my hand. The store clerk was apprehensive for separating the pup from its mother so early. He believed that we would have severe difficulties.

He was wrong. Blackie is fourteen years old now and has been my closest companion all that time. He gives me company and unconditional love. I can't desert my family, it means too much to me. I received so much, but have given nothing back to them. This hurts me deeply.

I still have to live here

Things have progressively got worse. The drinking is causing a lot of trouble within the home. My wife is having a difficult time coping through it. The finances are at an all time low. Yet, I am still in my downward spiral without any slowing down. I continue to drink and jeopardize everything I worked so hard for.

Work is being slowed down to a crawl. Deadlines are fast approaching, and I am nowhere near completing the work. The drinking has taken control of every aspect of my life including when I eat or sleep. It controls it all.

All of this is happening, and I still cannot quit. The overpowering need to disappear in my own little world is more important than reality. Your world does not have the peace and tranquility that I strive for. My world offers all of that and more. I become numb to the outside, which blocks the realities that haunt me.

It is this solitude that keeps me content and somewhat happy. I slip away behind the folds of darkness and disappear. My troubles disappear, and I am left feeling free from the outside.

Even though I feel this contentment, it is a selfish act for I seek this refuge at the cost of others. The family finances feed my habit until it is extinguished, leaving my wife and I destitute. My poor wife is left to fend for the household on her own rather than as a partnership. I have abandoned my friends and family. Nothing good really comes out from this behaviour except for selfish reasons.

My wife, councillor, and I have agreed to take action against my demons one more time. This time will include the detox program and a residential rehabilitation program at the rehabilitation centre. This is a comprehensive four-week program based on the twelve steps. I have to stop alcohol from destroying my life. I am very lucky for I have a very supportive family and system behind me. I have my wife, doctor, councillor, and others standing by my side every step of the way.

Even my drinking partner is on my side for recovery. He wants to see me succeed and beat my demons. He is still willing to be my friend, but will willingly stop drinking alcohol around me and prevent certain tempting circumstances.

As you can see, I'm much luckier than most people in my circumstance. I still have people who love and care for me. That makes all the difference in the world. I have people that will stand by my side through the thick of it and never stray. Many people have no support to help them through the rough times.

I have so much going for me. I have my book that I published. There is a second one on the go. I have a company that caters to the mentally ill and a newsletter, which is distributed on-line, and around town. I have a loving wife and dog, all in the security of our own home. There is lots of food in the house, so we will never go hungry. I am an extremely lucky man; I just don't realize how fortunate I really am. I take for granted the many things that most people would die for.

Through my writer's club, I have made several new friends that I adore. They are an intelligent bunch of people who have suffered similar experiences. Their stories are informative and enlightening. My company is currently working on producing a poetry book written by one of the members in the group.

To proceed with these plans, I have to remain sober. That is the only way it will work. There is too much work involved to allow it to be inhibited by my drug. I have slowly made a name for myself and am progressing at a steady pace. The one book is near completion now and will be ready for print in the near future.

Everything is going well, and I still throw a wrench into the works by continuing to drink myself to a stupor. If I am not careful, I could find myself on the streets in less than six months. It is a delicate situation; I am teetering on the edge of disaster. Even with this impending doom over my head, I can't seem to stop drinking and move ahead in my life.

I have to stop, and I don't know what I'm waiting for. I know I have obligations to my work and I have to consider those facts into a working program with my rehabilitation. I am in the process of wrapping up my work into a nice package so that I can take five weeks leave of absence for rehabilitation. As long as the other parties agree that my work is equally important, there should be no problem adhering to the plan.

Slowly, I am accepting the fact that I need help. I did feel very good when I quit last time. My health and everything about me improved tenfold. My work took off by leaps and bounds. I had energy and determination.

Even now, I am improving. I do more around the house and do more work for the company. I am gaining self-esteem enough to try rehabilitation one more time.

Of course, this has not been done alone; I have a great support system. This is the key to success. I don't particularly want to go away for a month, but if I have to, I will. There is a wide range of support available for people like myself. The decision is always up to us as individuals. There is counselling, support groups, detox, rehabilitation, and more. The choices are there. All we have to do is make one and work hard at it.

Perhaps, after I straighten out, other problems will also correct themselves. This is true financially, and the relationship between my wife and I would also improve. By changing one thing, the whole world opens up for me. While drinking, all the doors are closed and my choices are limited.

Writing my thoughts on paper is also therapeutic, and important to my well-being. It gives me a chance to freeze certain thoughts and think about them before writing them down. Thoughts come by in milliseconds, you have to choose one of them to decipher. The brain processes thousands of thoughts; very few actually are examined closely.

Writing can help with making a decision. When I was thinking about stopping my addiction, I wrote down all the reasons for quitting. Then, I wrote all the reasons for continuing my present course. I compared the two lists to make a decision on the outcome. I thought about those reasons, it came to a realization that the addiction was harmful to my well being.

The reasons for stopping out weighed the reasons on the other list. I rationalized these thoughts through the writings; I came up with the proper choice. This gave my brain enough time to decipher those reasons and process those thoughts into an action. Now, I am ready to face those challenges.

Denial and the realization that your present course is not in your best interest is the stepping stone to recovery. Once you accept that you have a problem, only then are you ready to face the music. You have accepted defeat from this addiction, and now you are ready to make a change in your behaviour. You have hit your ultimate low; there is no other place to go than up. Seize the opportunity and accept those changes into your daily living.

Through this writing process, I am building my confidence into making a change. I now know I have a problem and the reasons for that change. Accepting it now opens the doors for more choices.

Journals or memoirs are a great way to decipher those thousands of rambling thoughts. Try this, and you will be amazed at your accomplishments and progress. Professionals recommend writing as a form of therapy. It makes you sit down and think out your present situation and what you would like to change about it.

I can't live in the darkness forever. I have family and friends that need me here in your world. I have to build my inner strength and face these challenges here instead of walking away from them and hiding. My wife is opening up to me, and it is wonderful. This is all I want. I want to love and cherish her till the end of time.

She is an exceptional woman who appreciates the slightest thing from me. She is so happy if I have dinner on the table for her when she comes home late. We really do love each other very much. Sometimes, I wish we were a little closer, but that can also change with a little effort. It could be as simple as renting a movie and eating popcorn on the chesterfield together. It is the little things that matter.

My wife is quite easy to please. If I can do anything for her, she appreciates my effort. I get great pleasure seeing her smile and being happy. It makes me feel really good inside. This is where my real home is, and I have neglected it for so long. My life should consist of me being by my wife's side at all times through the good times or bad.

She has certainly suffered through the bad times with me, and yet she is still here. I don't know of any other woman that would have stuck around as long as she did under the same circumstances. This is the power of love.

Even though stricken by illness, I am a very lucky man. I have my own house, a loving wife, and a dog. I have family and friends who care about me. I also have the best support system to get me through the rough times. Fortunate to have all these things makes me humble for many people have nothing but their street family where addiction runs rampant.

I have to learn to realize how lucky I really am. I have food in my stomach and a warm bed to crawl into at night. I tend to demoralize myself thinking that I am the only one, but that is false. Millions of people have it far worse than I do. I really have nothing to gripe about. Although my life has, at times been traumatic, people do survive. It is time to count my blessings and move onto the future.

However calming is the darkness, I must refrain myself and face reality. This is where I belong. There will be a time when the darkness will be ready for me, but not now. I have to take care of things here and now. My wife requires me to be by her side, and I have to live up to those expectations.

This will take a lot of effort on my part to leave behind the darkness. I have learned that the time is now. I have to release myself from its grip on me and walk toward the light. My friends and family wait for me there.

I have my work and my determination to see it through. This is what carries me to the next day. My goals and ambitions are slowly coming true. Everyday, there is just a little more progress. With hard work and a little luck, I should achieve the goals that I have set for myself.

The addiction, however, is a very powerful force to overcome. The darkness captures the soul and tightens its grip on me. I don't know how to break away from it. It is so overwhelming that I become subdued by its power. I am in the middle of two entities fighting for territory, and I am the prize. Whichever side captures my soul will become a formidable force to reckon with.

How do I choose? I have friends and family on one side, and I have peace and tranquility on the other. What is the right choice? Do I abandon my life on earth and enter the darkness for good, or do I fight for my treasures here on this planet? Perhaps, I should live for the present, because that is where I am at now. My wife needs me here with her, not having me stare aimlessly out into space.

I still have trouble staying in the present. Periodically, I drift out into space, oblivious of the realities around me. My wife catches me several times during the day outside the realms of reality. Gently, she gains my attention, and again I become more conscious of my surroundings. Sometimes, I think that it is getting worse than it has been in the past. It seems to be more often and for longer periods of time. I really don't know what is happening to me. As strange as it sounds, maybe my doctor can make out a diagnosis from it. Perhaps it is a psychosis that sometimes has bouts of hallucinatory or delusional episodes. It's not always that common, except in severe cases.

Not unless the diagnosis I received when I was twelve years old, which—was manic depression/schizophrenia—may still be correct. I think only a doctor can help me discover the truth.

I still cannot find my strength and the will I once had. I had desire in my heart. I worked around the house, did chores, and was very productive. I have since lost that will. Nothing matters anymore. I lost my pride and all other attributes that orchestrated a normal healthy lifestyle. Now I am a useless tit on a bull. It is very degrading, and yet others are much worse off. I just don't care anymore like I used to. Even my physical strength has weakened.

I lost my spark for life, and it deeply hurts me. I don't know how to get it back. There is sludge in my veins. The fire in my heart went out years ago. It seems that there is no reason to push myself any further—my efforts are futile.

I don't understand it. My wife is thrilled with my accomplishments around the house or having dinner on the table. That should be enough incentive to carry on with projects around the house. Yet it does not seem enough like it used to. I was a great worker; now I can't work myself outside a wet paper bag.

Something happened five years ago that robbed my soul. I have no belief in myself. I wish I knew what the hell happened to me. I used to care about life, and now I don't. My health is no longer a concern. Perhaps, that is the time that I believed in the darkness. The time frame fits. That is the time my life on earth was extinguished.

That is also the time I became a severe alcoholic. Maybe, it really is the booze that robbed me of my life. I was so happy before. Now, I feel my pleasure by drowning my sorrows. That must be it. It's the fuck'n booze! Even when I quit for eight months, there were severe changes in my behaviour. I was happy and full of life, and now I am dead inside.

I know exactly when it happened. I just finished painting the inside of the house when I started to go into a depression. I then started drinking rye. Within a short time, I was drinking nearly forty ounces a night. From there it progressed to a two year drunken bedridden depression, and I never recovered. The depression went away, but the alcoholism stayed. This is where I am now. I am an alcoholic, and I need help.

I have to do it for my wife and family. They mean too much to me for me to neglect them. I still don't care about myself, but I do love my family and friends. Being dead would be too easy, even though that is what I really want. Am I scared of living and want the easy way out or am I selfish thinking that it is better on the other side? What the fuck is happening to me?

It is a bitter battle within my heart and soul. I am going to go against the grain and use my mind for logical reasons or will I follow my heart into darkness. Both forces are equal in strength for I am unable to make a clear decision. Both entities have assets worth pursuing. It seems, however, that with a lot of hard thinking that the best way to go is to rationalize the situation rather than following a whimsical dream.

What are my goals and what will get in the way of those goals? There is one thing that can stop those dreams from coming true. Of course, I am talking about the deadly elixir, alcohol. In an instant, it can wipe your life out. Without it, the sky is the limit. You can literally feel better on the first day of sobriety. Imagine six months, a year or ten years of being clean. Your whole life would change. That is financially almost forty-nine thousand dollars at the ten-year mark that you would save on booze. Of course, there are many more benefits than that.

What would you do for an extra fifty thousand dollars? You would save your liver and avoid other health risks. Your family would be happy and secure knowing that everything is all right. The benefits are enormous, yet we still sacrifice these things by buying another six-pack.

We believe we are using it as a medicine for our illness. That's bullshit!! We are doing nothing more than numbing the feelings for a few hours. There is no medicinal value at all. Just because you don't feel those feelings, doesn't mean that they're not there. You will have them return again the next morning.

You have a choice of facing those feelings and dealing with

them or numb them all over again. Once you have come to realize the facts, then you will be able to make the proper choice.

The big trick is staying sober long enough to logically make a decision. You can't do it under the influence. Drugs alter your thought process. It is impossible to make sound decisions while using. Some drugs also impair your motor skills such as alcohol and marijuana. These are the same problems that I face everyday. It is a Jekyll/Hide persona. My mind says, "No" and my drugs say, "Yes! Use me! Abuse me!" It sounds like a hooker on a Saturday night. Who can put off a good time?

Like me, many people need outside help. It is true that a mania will make you socially at ease, which may draw you to activities such as a bar or party. There is a trick you can use when you feel that urge. Eat something. It will stop the urge. I'm not sure why it works, but it immediately turns me off my addiction. It doesn't have to be anything heavy, just a light snack and the craving will go away. I'm not sure if this works for all drugs, but it does work for alcohol.

That little trick has also worked for my friends, so it is not just me who feels the affect of food diluting the urge to drink. In many cases, the food makes them tired. If you have been drinking and you eat something, there is a great chance that you will not continue to booze it up. This may not be the case for everyone, but it works very well for me.

I am desperate to try anything to help myself from grabbing another beer. I still have to live here. I might as well make the best with what I have and move on. I do have a choice. I want the best for my wife and that will mean that I have to be sober to enjoy that happiness with her.

With the writings, I have made my choice. Once I make up my mind to do something, there is nothing that will get in my way. A few weeks ago, I saw my drug rehabilitation councillor and even she remarked that I was quite ill at the time. She said, "Last time, you were only a shell of the man I normally know. This week you are alive, groomed and made significant changes in a short period of time." I have gone full circle and have decided that I will go to detox and an alcohol rehabilitation centre in the New Year.

Through my writings, I have weighed the situation, dissected and examined it to come up with an answer. I have now accepted the fact that I need help, and I am ready to work through these problems. In my heart and soul, I am committed to make things happen. I am ready for the challenge.

I can't seem to make a decision very quickly. It takes me several weeks of soul searching to build the confidence required for such a challenge. This is actually a fast turn around for many people take years to make such a life altering decision. Yet, there are thousands more who don't even get that far. So, in actual fact, the three weeks it took me to change my life around came by quite quickly. I only stayed in the contemplative stage for a few weeks. Now, I am ready for the active phase.

This chain of events happened much easier this time around for I have already been through it once before and was educated on the various topics related to alcoholism. Knowing is half the battle.

I don't expect to learn that much during that time for I have already been through an extensive program for addiction. The twelve-step program, however, is different for me. Apparently, they do the first five steps with you and then you are to continue on your own. I personally do not believe in the program, I think it is brainwashing rather than a cure. I don't believe in ninety meetings in ninety days, nor do I believe in their preaching.

Those are my personal thoughts. God has nothing to do with me stopping drinking; the strength comes from within. They believe that is the connection. It is you who makes the decision and the effort. You are the one who is going to struggle through the pain and agony. The cravings belong to you and no one else. This is your challenge. I presume if you need an artificial belief to get you through, I guess that's all right, but don't push it on me.

This is my problem and my battle. Alone, I will face my

demons with or without the aid of God. Preaching belongs in a church, not at a drug rehabilitation centre. I have my own beliefs, and they don't particularly agree with any one religion. I don't actually believe that Christ died on the cross. I believe he survived his wounds due to the quick attention given from his loved ones, thus, the second coming of Christ. Amen.

Patrick J. Schnerch

Starting all over again

It is a new fresh start at life again. I have so much to gain and so much that I can lose if I don't succeed. There is so much riding on it. This is quite the stressful time for I know what has to be done, but in my heart I'm not totally sure if I'm ready. It seems that is about as ready as I will ever be. I will still have some doubt if I can do it.

Perhaps once I start my treatment, things will start to fall into place. I will slowly gain my confidence. I know that last time I went through a huge transition that lifted my spirits well above the clouds. It felt that I hit rock bottom and that there was no other place to go but up. In a way, that was very true. I was in detox. You can't get much lower than that.

Now, I'm starting all over again. It seems to be a large obstacle that I must overcome. I do have goals and dreams for the future. I cannot accomplish those things if I am intoxicated. I need my full attention to make them come true. My work is far too important to be jeopardized by my addiction.

I am dedicated to help people like me to live happy and content lives. It is possible to soar above all odds and become a productive member of society. This does not particularly mean working for profit. Many people are unable to do that. Living on their own and taking care of themselves is a big achievement and should not be underestimated. This saves taxpayers millions of dollars in taxes.

Some volunteer their services and give back to society. The treatment, if adhered to, can be a Godsend to people living with mental illness and or addiction. Properly treated, they can go through life as well as their neighbour.

I inform them of services and areas of interest that may be of need of their focus. Lack of communication is the downfall for many people. Not knowing about services available is very frustrating. These things are not advertised or posted on bulletin boards. Somehow, through the grapevine, you may run across some service that may be useful.

The list is actually quite long, except nobody knows of it. The newsletter identifies these organizations and describes their goals and the programs available. This is an excellent source of getting the word around. The service is free of charge to the public. The circulation is quite large indeed. Plans of expanding are in the works right now.

This is very important to me, and I must remain in top form to carry out the numerous tasks to fulfill my dreams. The company also works with authors who have small projects such as booklets, pamphlets, and work with publicity. This keeps my days full of activity. Working long hours requires stamina and endurance. Drinking would destroy all of that and more. I wouldn't be able to deal with people or withstand the stress of deadlines.

I have to remind myself about what is important in my life. Booze is not one of them. I am working towards building a career, and I can't let anything get in the way of that. I am also busy building a content home life. Alcohol gets in the way of the things that I love. It is too easy too talk about it, but putting these words into action is a different story. If I already know what has to be done, why do I continue on my destructive path?

Last week, I talked to a man who is bipolar. He stated that he is not an alcoholic, but the social ease of the illness causes him to over indulge in pleasures such as alcohol. This is actually somewhat true, but in the course of over indulgence you are more likely to develop an addictive behaviour. You drink when you are manic, and you drink when you are depressed. That does not leave you much time for sobriety.

He was a well-dressed and groomed middle-aged man who credited his wife with his well-being. He stated that without her that he would be dead or on the street. That is the exact same position I am in. The only reason I can mingle with the public is due to my wife's constant baby-sitting of me. Otherwise, I would be a bum on the streets. She tries very hard for me to get into routines and try to make me take better care of myself. These attempts can prove to be futile at times, but she lovingly continues.

She only wants the best for me and to fulfill my promise to her to live a long life together. I want to do that for her. I owe her at least that much. I would also like to be successful in my work. Being out of employment for so long has damaged my self-esteem. There is no reason to brush my teeth or comb my hair. Self-pride has been extinguished for years already.

When I was working, all of that was very important. Now, I don't care anymore. I need a routine and a reason for being. Things are getting better. My work is starting to turn a profit. I now have paying customers looking for my service.

My appearance is important again. I must represent my business in its best form. I now have two clients who require my service. Formatting material into a book is what I am doing right now. One woman wants a writer with a little writing skill to make her work more profitable. I can do both jobs. However, my health will be in jeopardy trying to meet deadlines. It will affect my attendance at detox and rehab. If I stay busy, perhaps I may be able to work my way through on getting healthy, by not leaving enough time for my addiction. This one job is quite elaborate for it requires ghost writing and editing. The problem that most people don't understand is that it is labour intensive and time consuming.

They don't understand the work that is involved and are usually surprised at the cost. I have to put my foot down and not do things for free. I am not business - inclined; I am too softhearted. However, I have to stop paying for other people's projects with my own money; it will kill me. I have to charge competitive prices. I am starting with my next project.

I believe in God and my fellow man. I am a true believer of charity. However, that is not the way to run a business. I have to learn to work within the parameters of society and keep the wheels in motion. I am a registered business. I am expected to work for profit. I had no income for the past three years to claim on income tax. I must put my beliefs behind me and conduct fair and honest business. I can still have my morals and compassion as an asset, but the bottom line is profit.

My work is important to people and that there is a demand for it. I am skilful in what I do, and I can produce. There is no reason why I should not get paid for my service. I have to learn to believe in my abilities and myself. I do have many hidden talents that other people do not possess.

Society has pushed me away from the normal work force because of my disability. By looking at my work, you do not see a disability, but quality. Right now, I have a very happy customer. However, my service was free of charge. Further dealings will be charged in this particular project. I also provide services in publicity for my clients. I provide an affordable web page about them and their work plus contact and ordering information. I design, produce, and distribute brochures and business cards. I take orders, fill orders, and ship them to customers. There are book signings, event calendar listings, community paper coverage, newsletter coverage, and special events.

My services are many and often sought after. I tend to deal with people with real stories about life and tragedy, only to rise above and be fruitful again. People with disabilities are a very strong and determined sort. Physical, mental, or addictive impairments all block out a normal quality of life. These people are not expected to succeed in life, but become part of the system.

I like writing about success stories and the will of the human spirit. These people have experienced incredible odds and survived. Many of them are believers and rely on their faith for strength. Without hope, there really is no life. That's why I like working on the newsletter. I deal with real people with real problems. If I can help them to achieve a better life, then I will.

I had good people on my side for a great number of years, and I want to show my gratitude by helping others. I am in a position morally and mentally to give a helping hand. It makes me feel good inside that someone out there may benefit by what I am trying to do. I can do this by using the newsletter and by helping others with their literary projects. However, my charity has to stop somewhere before I find myself in ruins.

I have been meeting very interesting people in my journeys, and this is a benefit that I enjoy. They are people in need of help. I also use my morals and compassion for life to console my clients and give them hope. They appreciate the extra attention that I am able to give them. This does not come with the price; this is what I am. I thrive on helping people and on many occasions I sacrifice much of myself on every project. It is a passion of mine. I love people, and they seem to love me.

This is all I ever wanted. A little love and respect is nice to give out, but it is also nice to receive. I get that from my loving wife and my clients. This is certainly the way to recovery. Now, to remember that I am a useless tit on a bull if I am drinking, I must remember what is important in life. What decision would you make? It seems simple and obvious. However, mental illness and addiction are powerful foes.

I do get great pleasure from being productive and useful. Being needed by someone is a gift. Life is so precious and has so much to offer that it seems to be such a waste to rot at the bottom of a whiskey bottle. I have my demons, and I want my life back. It looks like if I can keep my head on straight, I will be able to achieve my goals and dreams.

It took thirty-three years to reach to this point in my life where I feel good about myself. If I work hard, I may become a provider for the family again. That would be a dream comes true. I would love to earn my keep again and become the man I always wanted to be. It seems that this may be possible despite my illness. I have learned to work through these conditions and survive. Now, I also want to earn a living. I am tired of being useless and battered by illness and addiction. I want to spread my wings and fly. After all these years, I am finally building my confidence and abilities to see me through. I will be the man that I want to be. I am loving, compassionate, and hard working. Too bad I also like to party hard as well. At least I am able to separate work from pleasure, which for many years I was unable to do.

I would try to work and drink at the same time. That was defeating my purpose. At least I realized that this combination does not work. Very little progress was made, and my abilities were severely damaged by this. My creativity suffered immensely. I now work for long hours without distortion. Now, to make my life full again, I have to quit completely. This is the only solution, and I know it.

I am slowly making my changes for my new transition into a healthier life. One day at a time. I owe it to myself. Growing everyday and learning as I go is a healthy way to encounter life and its little treasures. The alcohol is a terrible depressant and has a horrible affect on my mental health. I never realized how substantial its effects are on me. I was clouded by confusion and illusion. I was thinking that it was all right to feel that way. Even my writings were depressing while drinking and working.

Today, there is a future ahead for me. I have my place to hang my hat. This is where I really belong. I deserve to live among the living and not the darkness that has possessed me for so long.

I have to live for today in this world, not any other. My clients are counting on me to do a job for them. My wife expects love and respect, and I am willing to give that to her. My readers expect me to be on time with the newsletter. There is so much to do, and I am enjoying every minute of it.

How could I have been so foolish thinking that everything was fine just the way it was? I'm now facing reality and its hardships, thus, opening my eyes to the real world. I see things at face value. A drunk is a drunk.

I am seeing things for the very first time that eluded me for all those years. I am in tune with life again. It all has a purpose now. So much time has passed that everything is now all brand new and somewhat exciting. I feel good about myself waking up in the morning. I am no longer saddened that I woke up to a whole new day. Just imagine how much better I would feel if I were totally sober.

When I stopped drinking for eight months, I was in my prime. Everything was going right. The business was building and establishing itself. My wife was happy for the first time in many years. Even my dog was happy at the outcome for he used to get the whole family to go for a walk. Money was not a problem. Then, why did I start drinking again?

That's simple. I was desperate, and I was starting into a depression. I told my doctor, and he did nothing. Soon, I was out of control, and alcohol entered my life again. I could not withstand the effects of the depression. Either I fall into the unknown abyss or kill the effects it had on me. I chose the latter.

I had no place to turn, but my old faithful friend, the bottle. At least I deadened the agony of depression to stop me from going over the edge. I haven't been able to stop drinking since. Now, I am feeling better mentally again, so it is time to take action against the addiction again. When I am healthy, I do not require the alcohol to stay in control. That is when it is easy to quit. There are no urges to desperately calm down or fly into a party mode. Everything is quiet.

These urges are irresistible. It seems that I cannot refrain myself any longer; my back is against the wall. Panicked, I will resort to anything to control the situation. I know that I am making a big mistake, but if the situation is not controlled, even worse things will happen. At least when I am drunk, I am usually quite harmless. I may make a fool of myself, but no one gets hurt. It is the lesser of the two evils.

The big trick is to remain healthy to avoid such things from happening. This is usually not the case. The doctor seems incapable of controlling my moods when they change. The lack of control is the cause of all my troubles. I am scared, for I don't know what I am capable of. So, I take action with my own hands.

To make the system work, the mentally ill need affordable medication and a compassionate doctor that understands the level of stress their patient is under. That doctor should then be able to evaluate the situation and hospitalize the patient until the danger passes. However, because of the medical system crisis, hospitalization is only a dream. Suicidal people are sent back into the street with prescription for drugs that will take six weeks before they feel the affect. There are no words of encouragement or guidance. Your ten-minute appointment is over and then you are fed to the dogs. Crippled by despair, your addiction is your only answer.

My doctor does not listen or believe my pleas for help and dismisses me. I am left alone to fight my battles, and then he gets angry when I do things my way. There is no pleasing the man. There is not much covered in a five or ten minute appointment. I have never been able to express my thoughts and feelings in those brief encounters. Other than the medication, my treatment is useless. Even the medication does not work all the time. I still have depressive and manic episodes.

I need relief from those tortures, and I find it at the bottom of a beer mug. With these thoughts and feelings rotting inside of me, I am supposed to quit my addiction and become instantly cured. This is apparently my own doing, according to my doctor. He promises a life of bliss if I stop drinking. He's a damn dreamer. My doctor has no idea what it is like to be ill. He just knows what the textbooks tell him. You have to feel it to understand. Living day in and day out, not knowing if you will survive the day is normal practice.

The hell is still there if I drink or not. Only when I am well can I hold off the addiction. The doctor does not listen to this. The alcohol is the problem and that is his diagnosis. Eight months of sobriety did not mean a thing to him. That is expected of me. I expect him to keep me healthy so that I don't drink. He has not done that for me, and he is the one who is mad. I should be furious at him for I worked very hard at my sobriety. When I needed help, he failed me.

Now, I'm drinking like a fish and everyone is pointing the finger at me because I failed to remain sober. At least my wife understands, and she is coping with me. It is hard on her, too. She has to act as a banker and police officer. She makes sure that I don't have access to money, and makes sure that I stay out of the pub. That is a big sacrifice, because I have a lot of friends in there. I'm not even allowed to drink soda and be with my friends. I am totally cut off.

I presume there is a way around it. I can always invite them to my place for dinner. That would be acceptable to my wife. We could even have beers and have a nice time. The bar scene is out. I understand my wife's point of view though. I am terrible with money now that I am ill. I spend it faster than I get it. It just has to be this way. That's why we came to an agreeable arrangement that both parties were happy with.

I'm not terribly fond of the strict restrictions, but I know why we have agreed upon them. It is in the best interest for both of us. We have to save money and that's that. If I'm to live on this earth, I have to work hard toward staying here.

I have to learn rules, regulations, and routines all over again. It is like a whole new world. I am no longer a free agent. It's nothing like the world of darkness where there are no rules. Consequences of my actions were never thought of. Actions spoke louder than words. My own pleasure was all that mattered. I just can't do that any more.

Now, I have responsibilities to other people. I am expected to act in a certain way. I have meetings and deadlines to keep me in the paces. This is a very good thing for I now have a cause. This is a great way to help me into my transition back into your world.

The darkness feels so real—it is almost frightening. I have lived in the shadows for most of my life, and now I see the light at the end of the tunnel. I am most positive that another dimension actually exists, that is the only explanation of my experiences within the darkness. It is much too real to be a delusion or hallucination. There has to be an explanation.

I exist in this world while sober and awake. I can easily enter at will. It is so inviting that it is very difficult to resist. Somehow, I have to stop myself from entering and live for today. It is so peaceful and free that it becomes intoxicating like a drug. The urges to enter are also difficult to refuse. While under the influence, I can reside within the darkness for hours, days, or years. This is what I am truly addicted to. I'm addicted to freedom. The illness no longer exists in that world. I am at peace with myself.

With such a powerful entity, it is a struggle to stay within reality. I have to battle very hard to stay within your realm. Somehow, I have to stay within the parameters of reality and abide by the restrictions of your world. Freedom is a difficult thing to ignore. The tranquility is overwhelming. It is a sanctuary away from the grind of daily life. This is where I can rest and recuperate from the chaos of living on earth. I regenerate here and then am able to re-join the living for another day.

How do you resist such a temptation? Why would anyone want to stay within the refines of reality when happiness is just on the other side? Yet, I'm not supposed to go there. It is a restricted area, and most people are unaware that it exists. It does concern me that my illness has taken a turn for the worse and that I am traveling the long road to insanity. What would happen if I could never re-enter reality again? I would be institutionalized till the day I die, but I would be happy.

Unfortunately, my family would be distraught at the outcome. They would be left to continue on their own while I was residing in paradise. This is a scary thought for it seems that this is the direction that I am headed. I am afraid that such an event is likely to happen if there is no intervention. I am thinking that being locked up in a rubber room would make me be happy. That is delirious thinking that I have to resist at all costs.

I need my wife, home, and life on earth. I have to stay here. Even while describing the darkness in this chapter, I was swept away from your realm. It is becoming problematic, for it is happening more often and for longer periods of time. This happens even while I am sober. When I was drinking heavily, I did not realize that something was not right. I welcomed the retreat and induced it with alcohol. Now, I can't stop it.

I fade in and out throughout the day and am becoming very disturbed and frightened. I'm afraid that the condition is going to take over my will of living in reality. I didn't know how important that my life within the living really is until it is almost gone. Now I want to live here and not go back to the darkness that consumes my heart and soul.

I am awake and sober at this very moment and I feel my life slipping away through my fingers. This is very wrong, something is happening to me and I don't know what it is.

Patrick J. Schnerch

Panic

I was so distraught with the last two pages I wrote that I printed them and showed them to my wife. She said that once I get an idea in my head that there is no way of changing it. She believes my doctor that I felt bad about myself at an early age and now I have come to accept it. That is not true; in fact I found an escape from feeling bad about myself. It may be distorted from reality, but it helps me keep my sanity.

My wife believes that I actually have a very little grasp on reality at all. She is amazed that someone asks me to do something and I jump on it right away with both feet. This upsets her because she is angry because if she asks me to do something, months will pass by without action. What she fails to accept is that these things I do for people are paying jobs worth hundreds or thousands of dollars. What would you do? Fix a gutter or ghostwrite a book worth three or four thousand dollars? I put my time and energy into my career. Household chores do not rank very high when you are talking about a lot of money.

This does not mean that I am insane for having an interest in money and a better life. This is common dog fuck. That would mean that all of society, including her herself, is insane for going to work every morning. There are many jobs around the house that have been put off by her as well for she has priorities. I also have priorities. I want a career again. I want to be productive and prove my self-worth. This is not the perception of an insane man. I have gone years as a, "Honey, do this." It did not help me feel worthy; I felt like a slave.

I have done a lot of work around the house in the past without any recognition or gratitude for a job well done. I finally got fed up with the endless demands and decided to do something for me. Now, she is pissed. Money is what makes the world go round, not constant nagging. I will get to those demands when it is appropriate to do them. You do not silicone cracks during the rainy season for you are trapping the moisture inside the outdoor walls. You do not call a garbage removal truck, when you don't have the money to pay him. This is common sense. That is why I would rather work for money. I am no different than her, and I am the sick one.

What would you do? You could either rot the wall of your house or make three thousand dollars. According to her, if you chose the money, you are just as sick as I am. This is the level of insanity that I am in. I want money so that I can pay for the garbage truck. Face it. We are all a bunch of sick puppies for wanting a better life.

I feel that this complaint is futile. Agreed, I do have my problems and I work very hard to correct them, but I am not stupid. People automatically believe that stupidity is also part of a mental illness. My own wife believes that. A lot of people within society also believe that. I have a friend with schizophrenia, and she is the most out-going and intelligent person I have ever met. Her intelligence surpasses the shortcomings of the healthiest mind that I have ever been involved with. She has served on charity boards and organized fund-raisers for ill children. Her heart is so pure that she cannot decide if she should give a Christmas card or a gift to a person who mistreated her in the past.

Now, who is really sick? My own mentor has schizophrenia, and I love her dearly. No healthy person that I know of has any of the qualities and strength of this woman. She has earned my respect.

My own wife believes that I am a lost cause. The offer is still there. She could always marry a doctor or lawyer. She has no faith in my abilities unless I slave over a hot stove for her. My wants and needs do not have merit in this household. I am to cater to every little whim or expectation. I don't do that any more.

I want to work for a living, and nothing is going to get in the way of my dreams, not even my wife. She believes I should be locked up. I believe I should be in a suit signing thousand dollar contracts. She thinks that I have a serious problem. I think I am doing what you would rather do. I want to be successful and earn my way and pay my taxes like anyone else. Is this the thoughts and dreams of an insane man? I hate living off the system; I want my life back. Is this so desperately wrong? Is this the reason why I escape to my quiet sanctuary? I think it is a coping skill I developed.

If you didn't have sex for twenty years, I would certainly question your sanity too. The constant rejections, even for a hug or kiss, are very hurtful. I don't know anyone else who has to masturbate for intimacy. However, you have to remember, I am the loony tune. This is why I would rather sit in my office with a beer than watch Food-TV. She wants us to spend time together. That means watching a TV that constantly switches from one channel to the next.

That's why I didn't fix the remote control. This is not my idea of spending time together. She is upset that I go to bed early rather than watching Christine Cushing cook Mexican food. I wanted to do things with my wife for years, but have been unsuccessful in finding a common denominator. Now, we live separate lives. I have not felt love or support for a very long time and, of course, it has to be my fault. You have to understand my wife; she cannot do any wrong. Face it; she is the perfect human being. She is the, "One and only."

I am alone to face my troubles; to ease the pain I drink. Would you want to live like me? I fuck'n doubt it. There is a lot more to my addiction than what people really know about me. I could feel happy or watch Emeril Live with my wife. I don't mind spending time with my wife, but how we do it, erks the shit out of me. I'm a man. Cooking channels or the weather station does not amuse me. I'm sorry; I would rather do something useful like sleeping. However, we must blame this on the illness or me. You must remember who is perfect.

I get sick once in a while. Other times, I am in perfect health, but am not perceived that way. She does love me, and she has proven that on a thousand occasions, but there is a lack of understanding. I love her, not Michael Smith, the chef on TV.

I want to live a happy and normal life again and that means earning a dollar and becoming the breadwinner. Right now the roles are reversed and this does not sit well with me. I am not a maid, servant, or slave. I am a man. I am to work for a living, not vacuum the floor and do dishes or cook dinner. I grew up by the old school. Perhaps, my visions of life are distorted, but it has severely damaged my self-esteem. It seems that not only have our roles switched, but so did our sexuality. This does not sit right in my stomach. The only way that I remind myself that I am is man is when I take a pee. I may get slammed for my perception, but this is how I feel in my gut. My grandfather worked the farm; my father had a paying job. I only want what they had. All my male relatives have hard working jobs, and they wouldn't change a thing. They come home at night, have their dinner, and feel satisfied that they did well. I want the same thing, and I am not allowed to pursue my dreams. I cannot help but feel worthless. I don't believe that I am any different than anyone else. I want to feel worthy again. Being in the army was the happiest time of my life and now everything is gone.

I do what most unemployed men do. Drink booze. This does not make me a monster, but it does make the day easier to cope with. This happens to most men without meaning in their lives. I'm not insane; I'm quite normal. Of course, I am not perfect like some people I know, but I survive the best way I can. People are upset with me because I do not live up to their expectations. They want me to act like them, but do not allow me to pursue the things they are asking of me. If I had full time employment, there is no doubt in my mind that I would also be sober.

Under the circumstances, I am acting the same way most people would in my situation. If the situation changed, so would my actions. When people have time on their hands, a lot of them will grab a beer or joint and relax on the couch. I am no different. I just have a lot more time to relax than most people. If my day consisted of full-time employment, I would be no different than you. Yet, I am condemned by society for my situation. Give me back my health, and I will run fuck'n circles around you. Give me my job, and I will succeed.

I am a survivor. I use the tools available to get me from one day to the next. Live in my shoes and I will visit you in Eric Martin. I hate wearing dresses!

I may be a chauvinistic pig, and I apologize for that, but this is in my blood. I am supposed to work and be part of society. If I am to be normal, I have to be allowed to act normal. That means going to work every day from nine to five, five days a week. I will then feel good about myself and life will return to normal. Spending the day with Oprah Winfrey is not my idea of life. As you can see, I am not really any different than you. I also have feelings, wants, and needs just like you. Take them away from you, and you are nothing. I would give up my life in a heartbeat to live one day in your shoes. Society does not realize how lucky they really are.

Is this insane to think this way? To be normal and live life like everyone else is all I want. I don't know anybody who wants to be handicapped or on disability. It is not human nature. So, why is it any different for me? I will work again and be successful in life. I don't mean being rich in the wallet, but in soul. This is why I would rather work on the computer than rot out the wall in my house. The mentally ill and or addicted are not as stupid as you think.

This is not only my story; it belongs to thousands of people with dual-diagnosis, perhaps, millions worldwide. Mental illness is only a temporary condition that affects people some of the time. Otherwise, they can cope with life just as well as you can, if not better. It is a condition, not a disability, such as society labels it. Insurance companies, places of employment, and families believe that it is a disability. This is not particularly true. Many people live next to normal lives even with this infliction. They have just become stronger people because of it.

Their friends, family, and society as a whole have abandoned many. This is the honest truth. Imagine your wife having a heart attack. Instead of calling 911, you pack your suitcase and leave the house. This is what society does to the mentally ill. They pack up and leave. We are left to defend ourselves. If they don't abandon you, they ignore you and pretend that everything is perfect.

Society also believes in the perfect world. There are no such things as prostitutes trading their morals for drug money. People really are not hungry in their own city; they are just bums. The homeless are simply defiant against government policies. The mentally ill are just lazy people. As long as they are not in your backyard, the problem really doesn't exist. If they move into your neighbourhood, it causes an uprising, signing of petitions, new policies and laws, or evacuation. This is how society deals with them, or they put them in jail. Out of sight, out of mind concept is the normality of today.

Medication, employment, affordable housing, affordable day-care, affordable post-secondary education is a solution to many of society's ills. This is not acknowledged. Society would rather spend taxpayer dollars on outrageous costs for incarceration, institutionalization, hospitals, and government agencies. The money is misdirected to areas such as band-aids rather than cure the problem. Not everybody can afford the extravagant prices for a university degree. If this were regulated, employment problems would be a thing of the past. There is a demand for educated people; however, the resources are not affordable.

I want a writing course, but I don't have five thousand dollars. Proper medication and out–patient services will keep me out of jail or the hospital. If we had these provisions, food banks would not be required. Everyone would have a roof over his or her head. The government does not govern the areas that mean the most to their people. They throw the mentally ill in jails instead of giving them the proper care of a hospital. This happens in your own country. It's a fact!

I don't blame my wife for how she feels. She reacts the same way as everyone else, including politicians, judges, doctors, and a host of others.

No one listens to a mentally ill person and this includes his or her own family. I was expecting compassion and understanding when I told my wife about my fears and she gave me the third degree. I think even you would find yourself a rock and crawl under it if you were me. I want love, respect, and understanding. These are essential to healthy living. Right now, I am being forced to be sick by others who want me to be like them. Mentally, I'm fit as a fiddle. Emotionally, I am a wreck. So, I drink and escape from your fuck'n precious world; this is my way of dealing with it.

The only other recourse is suicide. I have tried living in your world, and I cannot seem to grasp my dreams. Rejected and alone, I must make a choice. Where do I belong? Obviously, I don't belong here. I am an unwanted pest waiting for his execution. I have already been hanged; I just didn't physically die yet.

The truth is that I love my wife till no end. I will never stop loving her, no matter what happens. It just feels so damn hurtful that I cry in my sleep. I want love so desperately—I can almost taste it. However, I am not allowed to have it, *I am mentally ill.*

The doctor believes differently. He believes that my whole problem stems from my alcoholism. Since that is the case, I have decided to stop seeing him or take any more medication. If that is my only problem, why should I poison myself with anti-psychotic drugs, anti-depressants, and mood stabilizers? Now, we will see for a fact if he is correct. This is the only way to find the truth. We will see what happens when I go through life untreated.

I think he is wrong and I am going to prove it, even if it puts me into my grave. It is party time! It is time to dance to the music.

It will be an interesting adventure. Maybe, I will spend the rest of my life in jail. It might be a short adventure at best. He believes that I have felt bad about myself since my childhood, and that I have learned to enjoy it. I only feel bad because I like it. It's all in my head. I am not mentally ill after all. All the doctors before him have misdiagnosed me.

I've been treated for mental illness for over three decades, and my only problem is that I am a drunk. I was foolish to believe all those doctors and specialists. This doctor I have now has the answer. I will live my life under the watchful eye of God. I have no other place to go. My hyper libido will return, but that is all in my head. The anti-psychotic medication apparently wasn't required. I must have had the idea of stalking innocent women in my teens. I don't recall anything like that, but this is the implication that I got from this doctor. My problem is substance abuse, not psychiatric.

Since I am not mentally ill, I no longer qualify for disability benefits. My only choice is to spare my wife's misery and move out. I have no other place to go but sleep in the parks and take to the streets. I'll be dead before my benefits run out. I will no longer be a burden to my dear, sweet wife.

I have come to accept my destiny. I am not going to take my wife down with me. Don't feel sad for me. This is the way God had it all planned. This is the way it is supposed to happen. There are no sad feelings or ill will. This is just the way it is.

In a way, I am relieved that it is all coming to an end. My wife will be free again. No more worry or pain. She deserves a lot better than a wretch like me. I am looking forward to my doom and will accept it with open arms. God may not want me, but that does not matter. I presume that for the time being I should continue as normal and wait to see what happens and deal with it then. Live it one day at a time until I am called for.

I will treat my wife with love and kindness. In the meantime, I will prepare and get the proper arrangements ready for when the time comes. I will not leave my wife hanging; I will prepare her for the inevitable.

Unfortunately, the withdrawals from the medication make you terribly ill. I've been sick like a dog for two days without any sleep or food. It will take some time for it to leave the system. Stopping the medication cold turkey is asking for trouble. You are supposed to wean off slowly. I don't care how sick I get; nothing is going to stop me from proving that ass-hole wrong.

I will continue to the best of my ability with the business until I get too ill to work. I love working and the newsletter. They both made me feel alive again. I am, however, willing to throw my life away to make that doctor realize that he made a big fuck'n mistake and he owes me big time. I will publish this book and make sure the world knows that ass-holes do exist, even if they are doctors.

What you just finished reading was me without three days of medication. I became so ill that I was bedridden. I had to go back on the medication. I was delirious with weird thoughts and actions. You can tell from the writing that I had totally lost it. I certainly don't want to sleep in the park or die. However, without medication, I was on a dangerous path. I will redirect that anger into positive energy thus working on schedule starting Monday morning. That will give me time to recuperate from that ordeal. It is obvious that the pills work. In a short period of only days, I was already climbing walls. The hyper libido did return only after twenty-four hours causing erotic dreams and erections.

I still feel ill with light headedness and head aches, but I should be back to normal after a couple of days. I'm already feeling much better than I was. I've slept and eaten something finally after a few days. That was a rough experience. I was willing to throw everything away. The fact of the matter is that I should just change doctors if I am unhappy with this one.

I should not let him upset me to the point of going over the edge. It is obvious that his preoccupation with the issue of alcohol is clouding his judgment on other issues as well. He is right though. I do have a character defect which stems from childhood, and I am an alcoholic, but I am also bipolar which sometimes gets bad enough that a psychosis appears. This was the diagnosis of the doctor previous to this one. In fact, this was the case for the last few decades. My psychosis was confused with me also having schizophrenia. Depression and manias can progress bad enough to cause psychosis, delusions, and hallucinations including hearing voices just like schizophrenia. So it is easy to make a misdiagnosis.

However, blaming alcohol as the sole culprit is wrong. I wasn't an alcoholic until six years ago. I was very ill previous to that, and alcohol was not a factor like it is today. I use it as an escape from the affects of the illness. Everyone wants to feel good, and alcohol helps me to feel that way again. That is why it is so addictive. Granted, I will feel better when I do stop my addiction. That is a proven fact, but it will not cure me of my illness.

My work is cut out for me. Being sober and healthy at the same time is sheer ecstasy. What do you do when you get sick again? I started drinking again because I had no relief from the illness. I found my own cure to the pain. The doctor never did it, and now he is angry with me.

What am I supposed to do? It is self-preservation. I think I do what millions of other people like me also do. It is called dual-diagnosis. Mental illness and substance abuse go hand in hand. It's not the right way to go, but many people seek the same relief as I do.

Better treatment is required to provide the relief to its sufferers. Then the addiction would not be such a factor. Much has to be done in the medical world. Doctors do not share the time or compassion for their patients in order to help them. Medications are not reliable to relieve the affects of the illness. Society turns a blind eye. The afflicted then turn to the only other relief they can find, and that is their addiction.

Drugs are expensive and require a lot of money. They will steal, beg, borrow, or prostitute themselves for their relief. Society then throws them in jail and treats them like animals. Only three provinces in this country put them in hospitals for proper treatment rather than warehouse them in penitentiaries.

It is common sense to treat the problem at the source rather than punishment for acting out from the condition of their illnesses. The justice system and society treat the mentally ill inhumanely and as second-class citizens. Charities and some government agencies are trying to cope with the demand, but much more has to be done.

Don't give us a bone and think that we will be content with that. We need much more. How would you like to be treated? We are no different—we are human beings!

Disgrace

Canada is not a third world country. We are one of the wealthiest countries in the world, yet we have thousands of homeless and hungry people in our streets. We have beggars, thieves, and morally deprived people inhabiting our downtown core. Mentally ill people are treated like animals when put in jail for misbehaviour caused by their illness. In solitary confinement, their condition worsens to severe depression, suicidal tendencies, and psychosis.

Priorities are very confusing in today's society. It is nearly impossible to survive with a two-income family. Housing is outrageous and unaffordable to many. Food prices are through the roof. Fuel, education, medical care, and the cost of living cause an influx of the working poor. If you have any illness, you are in financial despair. If you are mentally ill, you are swept under the carpet.

Granted, we are much luckier than most, but much more can be done. Of course the government pays for detox, and some rehabilitation programs and counselling, but they should. They receive billions of dollars a year in taxes from the number one mind altering drug in Canada, alcohol. Since it is so readily available and accessible, problems will occur. At least, since they are the cause of the problem, they are also paying something back into helping the people who fell through the cracks. Some cities, such as this one, have excellent facilities and treatment centres, but the waiting lists are sometimes quite long before you get in. They are, however, available to everyone. No matter where you come from, you can get help here by a registered medical staff. Thumbs up!

Charities are struggling to stay afloat. Social impact of people in need causes concern within the community that they reside. Discarded needles in the street, pot smoking and urinating in public are common complaints. Businesses are trying to gather customers into their establishment while their prospects are harassed for money or cigarettes. Soon the lease is expired and the needy are forced to move to yet another location.

Food banks and shelters are packed with people needing a roof over their head and food in their stomachs. The Salvation Army has a constant flow of clients seeking help. Out reach programs linking the street life with society are in demand. Churches are overwhelmed.

This small city has over seven hundred homeless people on the streets. That is absurd. Such a rich community and yet we have a serious problem with people not having a home. Hundreds more are being fed daily at local food banks. Subsidized housing has peaked and has a long waiting list. The list goes on and many of these individuals are mentally ill. Addicted and on the streets, they are cut off from society.

There are thousands more who at least have the necessities, but are living off the system. They have subsidized rent and food, but live meagre lifestyles barely surviving one month to the next. There are about fifteen thousand people on government disability for mental illness in this province alone.

The illness is real. It is a real problem trying to keep these people stable and productive. Many cannot work for a living and are forced to use the system. There are government agencies in place to help these people, but are not advertised or very well known. You have to be part of the system before these resources become available to you.

Once you are in the system, you will go through a transformation. You will change from living a productive and fruitful life to becoming a dependant of society. This is a culture shock to many people. They have a very hard time adjusting to the new way of life.

I found it extremely difficult changing from a productive member of society to a dependant of it. I lost my pride and self-esteem that I could no longer provide for my family and me. This was a severe blow, which I still have not recovered from. That is why my work today is so important. I want my pride back.

To live in society and to work shoulder to shoulder is a dream, which I am trying to achieve. There is a yearning to be normal and to stand tall among society. No more labels or discrimination. I want to earn the respect of others.

Many people also share my dream. Of course, there are some people who are plain defiant of the government and always want something, but never give in return. We also have to deal with them as well. Most of them have real reasons, such as mental illness and or addiction. Charities are the backbone to the community. They have the most resources available designed to help these people in need. This is where your charity dollars should go, not to individuals on the street. Most of them will use it on their addiction rather than food or shelter. It's not particularly their fault for doing that, but that is what a lot of them will do.

Every street person should have a caseworker to work on his or her behalf. They can make arrangements for food, shelter, and medical care as well as a small monthly income for those unable to work. They can arrange drug rehabilitation and counselling as well as psychiatric care. A link between society and the needy has to be established to provide a level playing field. We must get these people off the street and into homes. This is also a moral issue. They are God's creation, we are all different, but we shouldn't treat them differently. Some people treat animals better than they treat their fellow man. They deserve the same courtesy and respect as Fido.

Fido receives love, respect, shelter, and food. Why can't you treat James Arthur Lewis the same way? Is it because of his color, or belief, what he does, religion or what ailments he has? Granted, we all have a love for animals, why not humans? If a dog is hit buy a car, our heart sinks to a bottomless pit. If a man is shot on the street, we don't even seem to care at all. Our morals and values have declined over the years.

Love, morals, values, compassion, and respect are no longer taught in the family home. Society's heart is turning to stone. Greed and self-preservation is the mainstream. There is no compassion for your fellow human being. It takes an event like Christmas to make people think about charity. Think about it. They get one good hot meal, and then they are released back into the wet, cold streets where they will beg for their next meal.

Even Fido comes in at night to sleep in a warm house. Check out these charities yourself and see the people in the streets looking for a warm bed or hot meal. You should feel something in your heart rather than disgust. It could very easily happen to you.

People are so self-centered that anything that happens beyond the blinders is irrelevant. What they don't see doesn't exist. This is especially true for mental illness. They cannot see it; therefore, it does not exist.

I am a human with mental illness, but in your eyes, I do not exist. I am a nothing. I cannot work for a living, provide for my family, or socialize within a group. What good am I? I'll tell you how good I am. I have values, compassion, morals, heart, and intelligence to see me through. I also have God.

That is all I need. I do not need a big house or lobster for dinner or fancy clothes. I need acceptance. I am not a burden, but a man. I pay my bills and taxes, put food on the table, and provide shelter for my family. I'm just like you. I may be ill, but not stupid.

Learn to accept this. Not everyone has the same privileges as you do. It may be due to different circumstances, but they survive. They will not drop dead because you don't think they exist; they will always be there. One day, they will move to your backyard. What will you do then? Have them evacuated or deal with the problem that causes it? Out of sight, out of mind is not the answer. Face your problems and deal with them directly. If you don't like Shirley camping on your front lawn, find her a place where she can go. Don't push her off onto your neighbour. Help her.

A few phone calls and a heart will fix Shirley's problem and yours. Take time out for another human being and do what is right. Giving a helping hand is a gift far richer than money. Time and compassion is all it takes. Don't kick the puppy in the ribs, feed him, and love him, as you should any of God's creatures. Shirley deserves at least that.

Even the police in this province are working hard trying to

develop a SOP (Standard Operating Procedure) when dealing with people who have a mental illness. They were not trained to deal with such cases in the past. The ill were treated as criminals even though their situation could have been brought on by the illness. Sometimes force was required to calm down the person who could not control their actions. They may become boisterous, cause verbal and physical assaults, become defiant and suicidal. With the new SOP in place, the police are hoping for less fatal shootings when dealing with the mentally ill. The SOP will provide a series of non-fatal choices at their disposal.

The main reason why the mentally ill are warehoused in our prison system is because of the cutbacks and closures of mental care facilities in these provinces. Prisons lack the ability to handle mentally ill people humanly. Even judges want to get these people off the street by locking them up, rather than implementing medical care in a hospital. Many of those in the prison system will never rehabilitate if there is no medical intervention.

This could have very easily been me if I didn't have my support in place. Rather than writing about it, I would be living it in prison. I am very grateful for my present situation and not a day passes without saying, "Thank-you."

As a society, we have to learn that the mentally ill are people, too, with wants and needs. We have to change our line of thinking and become more social and compassionate towards all people by treating them fairly and with respect. People don't become poor or destitute by choice. They must survive, and they try to cope the best way possible.

Life on the street is much different than what the average Canadian is accustomed to. Morals are diminished and survival skills develop. I see what happens during my work for these people. Rules and regulations are commonly discarded for the sake of survival and may not be totally acceptable behaviour by the society at large.

Try living on the street for one week without any money and watch yourself demoralize. You will soon learn to live on animal instincts and act accordingly. After that week is over, then your views on charities and their clients will become more relevant in your life. You would return to your cushy lifestyle and home life leaving the cold barren streets to the less fortunate. You have to live it and walk in their shoes to appreciate the personal devastation that these people go through.

The streets are cold in many different ways. Not only is the weather near freezing during the winter months, but also the general acceptance of the public is also less than welcoming. When you see a prostitute standing on the corner in a revealing outfit during the winter, you believe that she is nothing but a whore. Get to know this person and learn that mental and physical abuse consumes most of her life.

Addiction, illness, and poverty are major factors. Lives are generally cut short and self-esteem and respect is lost. These poor souls even develop a hatred for a society that has not provided the simple basics of survival. Morals are sold blindly to sex crazed strangers. They too have no morals but do have the money.

Life on the streets is a vicious environment. Some are mothers and fathers that have fallen through the cracks of society. Unable to provide for themselves or their babies, they take to the streets.

Medication, affordable housing, affordable education, rehabilitation, clothing, food, group and one-to-one counselling are essential to these people. More money should be directed to these areas as preventable measures rather than dealing with the aftermath. Trying to fix damage that has already been done is usually very expensive and futile in attempting to correct the problem. You must deal with the situation on an individual basis and direct your attention to the sole cause of that problem and correct it at the roots.

To stop Jane from standing on street corners at the wee hours of the morning, she may need a psychiatrist and medication to control her bipolar disorder. Once controlled, counselling and a rehabilitation program thus reducing the need for big money from prostitution can address the addiction to street drugs. With social aid and subsidized housing, Jane can then up-grade her education for re-entry into the work force.

This does take time, but it is the only reliable and tested method of change. This situation is needed only temporarily until Jane is able to stand on solid ground again. This is much more humane that throwing Jane into jail for grand theft auto or drug offences. The incarceration is very expensive and does not address the problem at the core. It is strictly a punishment for a behaviour caused by illness and or addiction. Jane is sure to re-offend after serving her time for the problem, which caused it, has not been dealt with. In the long run, this becomes more expensive than providing her with affordable housing and the tools for a better education for a few years. At least, after rehabilitation, Jane is able to re-enter society and pay back her debt by working and paying her taxes.

It makes perfect sense to cure the ailments rather than punish it. People who are not rehabilitated become permanent members of the system either being locked up in jail or institutionalized for an illness never to see the outside again. If people would take the time and patience to lend a helping hand, this world would be better off for everyone. A bridge re-uniting people, as one society is essential to our future and the future of our children.

These lost souls need compassion and understanding. They are not only the homeless and hungry; they may be the lonely drunks in the dark corner of the bar or your neighbour, friend, or relative. They may be someone's son, daughter, mother, or father. Even with people around them, they may feel distraught and lonely yearning for love and understanding.

Communication and education will help close those gaps in your life. Listening is a powerful tool. Compassion is essential in everyone's life. You can be a father of five, husband, and businessman and still be alone and deserted. A connection or link has to be established. People need others for love and strength. Without this, life is meaningless.

If illness and or addiction play a role in your life, those needs are jeopardized immensely. Mental illness is not visible to the eyes and can be easily mislabelled as laziness or just a phase. You will find yourself not being taken seriously and your input regarded as of no value. This leads to poor self-esteem and lack of confidence.

Finally, all that you have come to love and cherish loses all significance. Family and friends are neglected and loneliness, self-pity and mere survival play an active role for your future. Either get lost in the abyss or change your negativity into a positive. You are always given a choice. It is up to you to make your own future whether it will be meaningful or wasted.

This does not mean personal wealth or power, but your connection with life in general. We must relate with others, understanding their plights and knowing that things happen for a reason. We were put on this earth for a reason. The paths we choose may have been already planned for us. We must have faith in ourselves and believe in our abilities to make proper choices financially, socially or morally. You don't have to believe in God to become a good, moral person, but you do need faith. Even force-fed beliefs are the building blocks to a moral life on earth. Whatever your belief, color, race or status in society, we are all the same. No matter what we achieve on this earth, we will only be left with our souls. Our hearts, minds, and souls are the true gifts that we all possess; material items are of no value in death. We are all the same, rich or poor. If God treats us the same as the next person, why can't we find it in our hearts to do the same? If you don't believe in God, there still is no valid reason to treat anybody better than anyone else.

People on the street deserve the same courtesy. They may be different in some ways, but they are all human. The mentally ill and addicted need your help to survive, not just at Christmas time, but also all year round. These people overwhelm the downtown core. Society sees it as an eyesore and wants these areas cleaned up. The people will just move to another location, but the problem will not go away. This out of sight, out of mind attitude does not work. The problem is still there.

You have to address the cause of the problem in order for change to take place. It is really just plain common sense. I am not about to change either until my mental condition is well under control. Once that is corrected, then sobriety is much easier to achieve. From there a domino effect of achievements are soon to follow. It is actually a very simple solution. So, why is it not done? I believe it is because the medical system is still unable to control the illness to satisfactory standards.

The person is at risk of addiction every time they fall ill. This is also common sense. Keep the illness away and everything will work out at the end. One thing to remember is that, if you are ill, it is not your fault. It is not due to a weak character or personality. When you are healthy, you can beat this thing. You will run into trouble when you get sick. That is the doctor's department. Tell your doctor everything so that treatment can be administered properly to keep you on track, thus not having to resort to self-medication.

Even the medical system treats the mentally ill like numbers rather than persons. This is degrading and hurtful when you are pleading for help and you are shoved aside. You are not taken seriously and your words have no bearing. Many times you are thought of as nothing more than an old drunk or drug addict without feelings. Not only are you fighting your illness, you are also doing battle with the medical system.

There is no compassion or personal knowledge of what it is like to be ill. They only go by what a book tells them. They memorize symptoms and prescribe a pill and that is their job completed. You are then pushed out the door into the world to fend for yourself. Alone and desperate, you turn to your addiction. Any relief is heavily sought after, even if it means sticking a needle in your arm or getting pissed in the pub. You are angry that your words had no meaning and that a five minute appointment and a piece of paper will make you feel all better.

Belittled and alone, you are faced with your demons. This is a demoralizing experience for you have fought a tough battle. You search for freedom of the illness and peace of mind. There is no light at the end of the tunnel so you numb it with your drug. At least for a little while, you have relief.

Then you think hard and believe the other people that you are nothing than a drunk or drug addict. Your self-esteem plummets and depression sets in. If you allow yourself to spiral far enough down, you will find that you have nothing left to live for. Your world turns black and the only safety you have left is from your drug. Nothing else matters anymore. Your family and friends don't exist anymore; their pleas and cries are not heard. With your mind numbed by addiction, your only chance of survival is to ride it out. Eventually, your mental health may improve enough for you to snap out of your depression and seek help or die trying.

Of course, there are severe repercussions of such behaviour. Divorce, financial debt, and homelessness are just a few of the realities that we face when we wake up. Soon, we are consumed with guilt and remorse, but unable to do anything about it. We are at the mercy of God.

The streets are my sanctuary. I feel a very close tie with them and the people who inhabit them. They all had lives before they took to the streets. They all had families and friends and now they are all gone. Some had good jobs or even careers, and they were taken away from them. Their drugs keep them warm at night and allow them to sleep till the next morning. If they wake up, the horror is still there to greet them.

They are frowned upon by society and even spit on or beaten up. They are mentally, physically, and emotionally dying on our streets. We turn a blind eye and look the other way, believing that they do not exist. Even though we live in Canada, stigma and prejudice still exists. This lives in every city and town in this great country of ours. It is our national disgrace.

Here I am

I was born an alcoholic among others just like me. My life was surrounded by booze through my teen-age years and into my military career. After the suicide attempt in the military and my diagnosis of manic depression, life lost its meaning.

One serious attempt to stop drinking lasted for eight months before illness struck again and put me back inside the bottle. Life was sweet while I was sober. Unfortunately, I am no better off now than what I was twenty years ago.

I am to go through detox and a residential treatment program for alcohol in the near future. However, this was a decision made by others and not by me. My heart is not into it. I am not ready to quit. I see this action as futile for I am not ready for it. Chances are that I will revert back to my old habits soon after my release from rehab.

Am I to die as an alcoholic or go through senility caused by the effects of long-term alcohol use? I still don't know where my future is heading. I don't know why I am spinning my wheels. I'm not even sure if my wife is willing to hold out much longer. It seems to be a dire situation with the exception that I do not care.

I really don't see anything wrong with the way I am as compared to what I used to be or how alcoholism affected my family in the past. However, there are times that I like to let loose and I have to control that. The meaning of alcoholism has two different characteristics as compared to what I grew up with and what I actually do. My wife sees it differently. She believes that I am totally out of control and I personally seen much worse. I know what a real alcoholic does.

My wife also knows about real alcoholism because she grew up with it in her own family. That situation is much worse compared to what is happening to me, yet she is all up in arms against me and not her own family.

I have to quit sometime, but not now. It will never work until I am ready. Going against my will only escalate further problems of defiance. It is my hope that my work will keep me occupied enough so that my use of alcohol decreases automatically due to my need to stay aware and conscious of making accurate decisions.

I am lucky in a way that my work has much more priority than what my drinking does. I have deadlines to meet and a heavy schedule. My work comes first before anything else. My problem lies with structure. Right now, it doesn't matter if I have a couple of beers while I am writing as long as I limit my intake or my day is shot.

If I can structure a proper eight-hour workday without drinking, my work will certainly be at its best form. Then if I make dinner and eat with my wife, I could later relax with a couple of beers and be much better off for it. That may even be more acceptable to my wife for I would also be cutting down on the amount I drink at the same time.

Routine is my biggest problem. My sleep and eating habits are greatly affected by drinking pattern. If I can structure my time effectively, most of my problems would rectify themselves. I usually still get eight hours work in, but I start anywhere from two A.M. to four A.M. By eight or ten o'clock, my workday is already finished, and then I start drinking. This is extremely disruptive. In the early evening, I am already in bed exhausted from the effects of a full day and drinking. This has to change. I still receive a fair amount of sleep at night, but it is very difficult to refrain from napping in the afternoon especially after having a few beers.

It would be ideal to quit drinking all together and work on my routine and schedules. I know there was vast improvement during my eight-month sobriety. I just can't find the strength or will in my heart to put those words into action at this time. I just don't feel ready for a change right now. I want to pursue such action only if I have a chance of succeeding. I don't want to fail again, and failure is imminent if I was to stop now.

I have to do this for me, not do what everyone else who wants this. I have to make my own decision when I am ready to quit. Bitching and nagging does not do anyone any good. It just causes bad feelings towards each other. No one understands what it is like. Just because someone tells you to do something doesn't mean that this will be your instant cure to all your problems. It doesn't work like that at all.

I did quit drinking, but the real problem was still there. You have to address the other problems as well. I have mental and emotional problems, which must be dealt with. If you only work against the alcohol and neglect the other issues, you are bound to fail. You have to target the cause, not the result.

As it stands now, I do not have the support in place to make this a successful transition. Everyone is up in arms, but is not willing to go the extra mile. If this does not change, it would be better off to break all ties and go our separate ways. That includes everyone in the support system at this time. It seems to be fruitless on our present course; nothing is going to change if the real problems are not treated as well. The whole burden is left on my shoulders to change my ways, but no one else is willing to change with me.

Education is the key. Everyone is blinded by the alcoholism and cannot see the light at the end of the tunnel. There is more work than what meets the eye. If the need to drink were not prevalent, then there would be no problem. As it is now, I am better off to fight this on my own terms. When I deal with the other issues and am stable enough to stand on my own, then the drinking will be a thing of the past. It is a simple solution. You have to cure the real problem first and then worry about the after-effects. Not only am I fighting these conditions, have I also had to fight with the people who are allegedly trying to help me.

Don't give a thirsty horse a tablespoon of water and think that it will give you a full day of hard work. This is the same thing. Give me the proper treatment, and I will excel in life. The alcoholism is just an after-effect of the real problem. Many people find dissatisfaction in their treatment and often self-medicate to make them feel better. It just goes hand in hand with mental illness. However, this really pisses off the doctors for their hands are tied and are unable to treat you properly.

Some people do not seek professional help and continue to self-medicate. To a certain extent, it works. Unfortunately, other problems arise. Thousands of people continue this way. As long as they stay out of the hospital, all is well. It doesn't seem to matter that they pass out under the kitchen table or get thrown in the drunk tank by the police. These are only minor setbacks, which prevent major problems from developing.

I would rather be passed out drunken on the streets than stalking and raping a woman. I would rather stagger off to bed than do something I would later regret. I would rather get cut off from the bar than cause self harm. It is the lesser of the two evils. There is so much more at stake than just having a good drunk.

It's self-preservation. I'd rather sleep off a drunk and wake up with a hangover than fight someone and cause a disturbance. At least, it is only me who gets hurt. Being sober and out of control due to illness could be catastrophic. Sleeping peacefully in my bed is a safe alterative.

Those are some of the factors, which I would avoid at any cost, even if it meant that I remained a drunk for the rest of my life. This is scary stuff. I don't want to be hospitalized, institutionalized, incarcerated, or dead. I plead to anyone who knows how to deal with the situation any better. I have seen a dozen doctors in my lifetime, and none of them are able to relieve me of this anguish.

I am much better than I was in the past due to my present treatment, but I'm still not cured. The combination of treatment and self–medication seems to be enough to keep me out of hospital and trouble. It only seems that this may be about as good as it gets. I am productive, happy, and grateful for being alive. It really doesn't get much better than that. I may spend too much money on my habits, but it could be much worse. We are not hungry and we have a roof over our heads. We have equity in our home and have plans for major renovations next year.

We are thinking of the future together as husband and wife. We will be married for twenty-five years next year. Things are working out, despite my inadequacies.

My business is seeing activity this year and is building. My charity to the less fortunate is on solid ground. I haven't been sick for a year already. This is very promising. Content and happy is the main goal, and I have achieved it. I may like a couple of beers at night watching TV with my wife, but it is not the end of the world. There has to be compromise and acceptance. Face the realities and move on. There is a whole life to explore.

I tried living the way other people want me to be, but that was of no success. I have moved through life on my own and worked toward bettering it day by day. One day I will stop smoking. Then I will stop drinking. I just can't do it according to other peoples' agenda; it has to be on my terms for I am the only one dealing with it everyday.

No one can do it for you. It is a solo event. No amount of nagging or disgust is going to make things better. Life is not perfect, and we have to accept it. We have to make due with what we already have and live day to day. I want to make other people happy and proud of me, but on my own terms. I can't please everyone all of the time. I am not perfect, and I don't pretend to be that way.

People say that trying is just an excuse and that the only course of action is to do it, come hell or high water. I disagree with that philosophy. They may go full guns and fail anyway. It was obvious that it was not successful—it was only an attempt. They tried. They never succeeded.

The decision to change your ways has to come from deep within your soul. You may ask for help, but you are the only one that can make it happen. Advice and a helping hand are all well and good and you may find that essential, but it is only you who can stop your drug of choice.

When it is time for me to make my decision to quit drinking, it will be the decision of my mind and soul. I have to go into this with my heart. Failure is inevitable if it is anything less.

What does the future have in store for me? I do have hope and dreams, which this is something I have not had for over three decades. I want to make them come true, and I am willing to work hard to see that this does happen. With my wife by my side, I hope to have a fruitful and happy life together for a long time to come. I have come a very long way in life. Although life is not perfect, I am happy and content. That is all you can ask for, nothing else matters. Big houses, cars, and boats don't mean a damn thing. Kissing your wife goodnight means everything.

I have people in my life that want to take this happiness and contentment away from me. This is the best I felt in my entire life, and I am supposed to give in to their wills and wants. I just can't do it. I have tried my whole life to get to this plateau and it will be one hell of a fight before I give it all up. I love my wife and family with all my sincerity and I don't want to change that. I may die at a young age, but my life will be fulfilled with happiness and joy.

I am doing things now. I am making a difference in other peoples' lives. This is extremely important and gratifying to me. I saw a mentally challenged person take eight of the ten newsletters from the waiting room of a psychiatric hospital. She thought it was important enough to pass my information around that she drained their supply. This dear woman found something in my newsletter that put a little spark into her day. Even if it is only one person that I may help, that is all that I need to continue in my crusade.

There have been others as well. I am reaching out to these people and it is working. People are reading and understanding my work. It is not in vain. There is now a connection between my friends in need, and me. I will do anything in my power to make them smile for another day. This is my gift to them. I want my friends to have a full stomach and a roof over their heads and sleep in their own comfy bed.

All that I am able to do is give them hope and inspiration. Perhaps, my voice will help someone to make a change in his or her lives. There is hope. I don't have much, but it is a hell of a lot more than these poor people has that I see in my travels. It breaks my heart to sit in the waiting room of a psychiatric hospital watching my desperate friends reaching out for help only to be sent out onto the streets to defend for themselves. They grab their shopping carts and search for recyclable material to buy a hot cup of coffee. This is fuck'n heartbreaking.

I may have had my troubles in the past, but that is over now. There are people out there whose lives are disappearing before our very own eyes. They are dying on our streets and no one cares.

Maybe from reading my story, you will understand where my humanity and love for life have come from. This is where I stand today. I love my friends of need. Society has to change their ways. Jesus did it and so can you.

Love is what makes the world go round. Look in your heart and look to what is happening around you. Open your eyes and look. These are people. Most animals are treated better than we treat a mentally ill person. Animals also deserve love and security, but so does James Robert Baker or Shirley Agatha Jones.

This is my love and life. Please don't take it away from me. Don't take my love away; I cherish the way I am. Yes, I am troubled, but I have a heart and that is all I need. I received my heart from my dear aunt and uncle from years gone by. There are far more important stories to listen to or read than mine, but maybe this is a good place to start.

I have survived some challenges and yet there are more to come, but that is what life is all about. Everyday, there will be something new for us to face. It all depends on where your heart is if you are to survive or not. I am lucky for I have strong morals and values to keep me in check even in the most adverse situations.

It took many years to overcome my fears of my Uncle Adam, which later flourished into an unbreakable bond. He was a great man to whom I am forever grateful for being there for me. Even in his bad times, his strength and determination shone through. He learned from his mistakes and made the necessary changes. Those changes were dramatic for which the real man was revealed, not the alcoholic. Uncle Adam was a courageous man who fought and won his battle against alcoholism. I can only dream of having his strength and the courage to follow in his footsteps.

The later years of his life were fabulous. My aunt was happy with her life and was torn to pieces after his death. Yet, she, too, is a survivor. I owe those two people my life. They raised me in my most formative years to become a respectable and loving man. This is what I am and there is no changing it.

I want to stand tall in a crowd and not be labelled as a mentally ill man or alcoholic. I want to stand on my own two feet and provide for my wife like I used to. To be free of the system and become my own man with my own destiny is a goal that I am working hard towards fulfilling.

I want to be a man again. I have lost myself over the past three decades and am only now realizing my self worth. This will take time yet, but I do have the time and patience to wait. I let over thirty years pass me by. Another few years will not be tragic for the outcome will be beneficial to my well-being. Growing and learning about life all over again is exciting. I am making new discoveries everyday. This experience of discovering me during the writing of this book has been therapeutic and healing.

It has been a journey in which I have learned my lessons during my past. It shows you how impressionable children are from their upbringing. As parents, we are responsible for the guidance and teachings of our children. They learn from our mistakes and us. The environment in which we raise our children will have a severe impact later on in their lives. Children are very impressionable and will pick up things from you naturally. This is all the more reason to be on your best behaviour and teach them right from wrong.

We must protect our children and love them unconditionally. They will never stop needing us. I need my aunt now and forever. She will always be my mom. I phone her on a regular basis and keep in touch with her. I don't have the money to visit her, but I never forget her. I send her mailings of my accomplishments just to let her know what I am doing in my life.

What happened to me caused permanent character damage. Emotionally I was destroyed. I think my questions have been finally answered after writing this book. It has taken many years to understand what has happened to me. Those early years made up my character and personality. Unfortunately, this is where the damage was done. There has been a lot of negativity in my life, and now I am finally learning how to deal with it. It has taken my whole life to come to grips with myself.

Maybe today, there is a light at the end of the tunnel. I hope that in the future I will finally learn to love myself again. I lived with self-hatred for so long, it has become increasingly difficult to change my ways. I had no reason to love or care about myself. Hopefully, this is another change that will soon be established.

With all the love in my heart for others, I have always neglected myself. It is hard to restore pride when failure has been a major contributing factor to my life. I am feeling better, but there is still a long way to go before I become more confident in myself. My confidence has been shattered at an early age. It will take a long time to heal. You have to deal with the past before you can move on into the future. I am dealing with that now.

I am finally healthy enough to face my past and understand it. I have to live one day at a time, putting one baby step in front of the other. I have to heal before moving on with my life. There was a lot of damage done, and it will take time before I can learn to accept it. Only then can I start to work towards my future. That will be the time that I will be ready to make changes.

This book will be my closure to my past. This had to be done. I have to make peace with God and myself. With his strength and guidance, I will move on to new challenges and adventures. I believe I have taken major steps towards those goals and dreams. It is time to follow up on those dreams and make them come true.

My time is coming. I will soon be independent once again. This is very important to a man's self-esteem. The bad part is over now, and it is nearly time to carry on in a future that is yet to reveal itself. I haven't had a chance to prove to myself that I am a real man. I have a hard time convincing myself of that fact. I have not lived up to my own expectations. It is time for change.

I've been a little boy all my life, hiding behind the shadows, being too scared to face reality. The darkness has kept me alive till now. It is time to step into the light and face the world head on. Today, I grew up. I am now a man.

This journey to manhood has been a difficult one. Being middle-aged, I have finally come about to act my age. My childhood is over as of today. I don't need children to prove otherwise. I have now accepted my inadequacies and made peace with myself.

I am who I am, and nothing will change that. I am proud of whom I am and what I have done to get here. It was my editor who made me realize that my problem arose from my early childhood. It may have been my illness triggered by circumstances to manifest early in childhood.

The signs were there all along, but went unnoticed. I went through a large portion of my life not being medically treated properly until the inevitable happened. Feeling so bad and desperate about myself, all I could think of was suicide.

From the bowels of hell to happiness and fulfillment was a long winding road. Of course, this could not be done without the help from others. I owe my life and gratitude to all those who stuck by my side, especially my wife Kathy. If it was not for her, I would have been dead years ago.

What's happening to me?

I am losing my mind. I totally lost it. I told my wife that I was leaving her, and that I couldn't handle being a prisoner in my own house. I came up with a bizarre scheme to become a roommate only and not a husband.

I was out of control. I was crying for I love her so much, but I felt backed in a corner. My freedoms were taken away from me, and I snapped. I wasn't able to buy a cup of coffee or a lunch, and I was trapped in the house with no one to talk to. This was too much for me to handle.

My spending habits were out of control and my wife acted accordingly, but it had lasting effects on my sanity. I have to learn to stay in control if this is going to work. My wife is doing the best she can under the circumstances. I left her with no choice but to be aggressive with the money, but to leave me totally penniless without being able to buy a pack of cigarettes was too much to handle. I couldn't go anywhere or get out of the house for a while to clear my head.

I was insane yesterday. I almost called the crisis centre for help. I bought my own food and paid my wife money for my fair share of the sundries and food that I use. I was determined to end the relationship. I even took off my wedding ring. I was totally gone.

I drank to calm down and try to sleep it off. I feel better today than I did yesterday. Being a prisoner really threw me for a loop. This just does not work. It is my money, too. She can't cut me off totally. It is not fair. I also contribute to the household and bills. Not being able to buy a pack of cigarettes was the clincher. It was the last straw that broke the camel's back.

Now I have to be careful with the money I do have and not go overboard. She gave me my card back. I think I have a plan that will work out to satisfy both of us and save money at the same time.

I have to collect my thoughts. Yesterday I was very close to suicide. It was the steady flow of beer that saved my life. I became relaxed enough to go to bed safely. If I was sober, I am quite sure that I would've hurt myself yesterday and am in a psychiatric hospital over the Christmas Season. You see--there is a need for addiction when you are mentally ill. It is unfortunate, but booze has actually saved my life on several occasions.

Medication does not do that while you are in crisis. Alcohol calms you down instantly when you need it the most. If it means drinking until you pass out, at least you are safe. It is simply self-preservation and survival. When nothing else is there to save your sorry ass, at least there is booze. Doctors don't understand how desperate things can become. They believe a simple pill will cure the problem. I know from experience that while in crisis, this is not true.

There is no medication on the market to use if you are in danger. Where do you go? I thought of it yesterday, there is the crisis line. From that point, they take you to hospital and give you a drug that causes you to sleep off your troubles and enter a new day. It does cause you to hallucinate, but it works beautifully. This is standard procedure on admittance. I could have done that, but I don't want to spend the holidays in hospital.

I want my turkey dinner on Christmas day and spend time with the family. I don't want to be locked up tight for a few months until I recover. Even though my actions are not predictable, I still want to try to have a nice meal with my family. I don't care what happens to me after that, but I want that one special day with my wife. I just have to hold out for a couple more days.

With enough beer to keep me calm and in control, I am sure that I can survive. It is difficult to understand that such a drug is useful in preventing a disaster from happening, but it is true. When you are desperately ill, there is no other place to turn. Medically, there is help. However, this is usually lengthy hospitalization. We try to avoid those situations at all costs. This is why addiction is so hard to break away from, because in many cases it saved our lives.

We don't want to be hospitalized, poked and prodded. We want to live next to normal lives. Is it more important to comply with outsiders who don't understand or should we cope to the best of our ability? Granted, addiction is very difficult to live with, but when lives are at stake, what do you do?

Professionals detest addiction. If they had it their way, they would throw you on the street until you straighten out. They don't have the time to waste on something that they cannot control. They were trained in mental illness not alcoholism. Perhaps, that is the reason my doctor is so angry with me. He made this abundantly clear to me.

The thing is he has not been successful in stopping a crisis from occurring. He does not see his own inadequacies. He blames only the booze, and me other than that he does not give a rat's ass.

What would he do in a life and death situation? I will bet my bottom dollar that he would take that drink. Why am I any different? What the fuck makes him so high and mighty? This really pisses me off.

This is survival in its purest form. You do whatever it takes to save your life. If any of you were in a life and death situation, I am positive that you would do anything in your power to survive. This is not any different, but the battle is in your mind. This is the most dangerous place to be in. You are fighting valiantly against yourself.

You battle so fiercely that your head aches with pain. You shake and sweat with anxiety. Swirling suicidal thoughts inhibit your mind. Hopefully, you have the strength to survive. You cry for you do not see any hope. With knife in hand, what are you going to do?

I have lost my sanity for a couple of days. It was of real luck that I survived those two days. I took off my wedding ring and thought that this was my end. However, I could not resist the love and smile of my wife. She brought me back into reality.

Now, I am hoping for a nice Christmas dinner with her family. With all my sincerity, I wish that everything turned out for the best. I've missed several Christmas dinners in the past; I hope that this one is without event.

I lost my head last Christmas as well as becoming very ill. I wasn't even using alcohol at the time. I was sober, but still very ill. Suicide seems very prominent at this time of year for me. It is a very sad time for me. Boxing Day is worse, because this year it marks the fifth year since my dear uncle's death. This is a real killer for my poor aunt as well. I don't think she'll ever get over it. She truly loved him with all her heart, and he loved her. They were meant for each other.

Our giant teddy bear is gone, and we miss him dearly. He used to love Christmas because the family came to visit him. Mom made a great turkey dinner with all the fixings including Ukrainian and German cuisine such as perogies and cabbage rolls. It was truly a feast fit for a king. Dad was our king, and he was in his glory when everyone came over to eat on Christmas Day. He loved his food. I felt so sorry for him when he became a diabetic. He was hungry all the time because of this diet he was on. It was sad to see him eat this minute amount of rabbit food on his plate when he really wanted perogies and turkey.

He was a survivor. Uncle Adam fought to the very end. When it was time, he gave himself to God and accepted his death like a brave man. Sure, he was crying too, but he loved his family and he was going to miss them as well.

He had his troubles when he was a younger man, but he overcame them. My uncle was a good man. He scared me at times, but this was not intentional. It was the booze that was poisoning his tender soul. It is of no wonder why my aunt fell in love with this great man. He was a soldier, man, and my aunt's only true love. I miss him very much.

I can't forget my biological father for we had great times as well in the later years of his life. We used to walk up to the chicken place and Dad would buy dinner and beer for me and we would have a nice quiet time together and talk. Those were real good times. I learned later in life that he was a generous and compassionate man like my uncle Adam. We spent a lot of time together in those years, and he felt love in his heart again. He couldn't show it or say it, but it was there.

I think we made our peace with each other even though there were no words spoken. He was a very shy and quiet man. I honour his second wife for making him so happy for those years she gave him. We didn't get along too well together, but we managed to be at least very civil about it. We had our differences, but she loved my father very much. They were inseparable. I do owe her my gratitude for keeping my father happy for many years.

I don't think they meant any ill will, but sometimes it was not that easy to distinguish. They were very defensive about whom they allowed in their tight circle. They were quite wary of strangers or motives of others. Many times, it was unwarranted. They were not the easiest people to get along with, but my father and I along with a bottle of whiskey became true friends. The only way you could reach his heart was through his melted brain.

He took great pleasure sitting down with a bottle and me. It was the only way to get through to him, but he was happy. I can't take that away from him. I love my father unconditionally. I just wish that there weren't so many secrets. He knew I was weak, and he did everything in his power to protect me from getting hurt. He was trying to be a good protector, but he didn't know how to raise a child. The child has to feel love and warmth to embrace. Neglect and idle threats were damaging to the spirit.

It is Christmas Day, and I am paying my respects to those who I love that have passed on before me. This is my Christmas gift to the spirits that touched my soul so many years ago. I pray for their keep under God almighty.

I cannot forget about the living. I have friends and family whom I love deeply. I want to make this day special for them, especially my wife. I am a lucky and grateful man to have her by my side. I will help her today to get the turkey ready for our feast tonight. I will give her a kiss and a hug to remind her that I love her.

I will give best wishes to my friends and family either in person or on the phone. Today is a special day to remind us of the loved ones in our lives. I have much to be grateful for. I have people who love me, a roof over my head, and food in my stomach. There is no need for anything else. There is a warm bed to sleep in at night away from the cold and wet weather. I have everything I need.

It is time to move on with the present time and make each day count. The past has haunted me all my life. It is time to move on. Count my blessings and seize the day.

I have to control my sanity somehow. If I remember how fortunate I really am and forget about my troubled past, I should be just fine.

Take account of your lives. See things for what they really are and hold you accountable. It is only you who can make a difference. If you don't like the way things are in your life, you have the power to change them. This is true for me as well. There are things that I am not proud of. With God's help, I will have the strength to move on in life.

There is one woman who looks up to me as her mentor and I take that as a sincere compliment. She worships the ground I walk on. She hugs and kisses me and holds on tightly, arm in arm. She is a dear woman, and I visited her when she was in the hospital lately. That made her feels very grateful. I do have an impact on people. I really do matter.

She looks up to my bravery and how I battle my conditions. She absorbs my honesty and truthfulness and respects the fact that I treat her like a human being and not like a piece of meat. This woman loves my direct approach in my writing--again the honesty shines through. Donna believes in me and we share a kindred spirit.

I never thought that I have an impact on other peoples' lives, but I do. This was evident at my commencement from a drug rehabilitation program. The other members had a great deal of kind words for me, which I never realized was part of my kind nature. I also had an impact on them. Perhaps, my newsletter also touches other people as well.

It is candid and touching of the heart. I go beyond what a newsletter really is. I talk to people from the heart. It is our souls that we want to keep. My newsletter does that and more. It does more than just report events and happenings--it shares feelings. It is based on the truth and nothing more. It is a very honest publication.

We do make a difference as individuals. Together, we can move mountains. That includes addiction. It can be beaten. We have to believe in ourselves.

I understand fully that this is a very difficult thing to do. Especially when attacked by mental illness can this be very taxing. I was lucky to survive the last two days, and I don't know how I would have made it if it were not for the booze. It is a sad shame, but alcohol does work in certain cases. However, in many cases it is also the cause of your troubles by causing a drug induced depression. This was not evident at this particular time. I didn't start drinking until after the fact.

If we could only control our illnesses, that would be a blessing from above. I couldn't believe what was going through my head. I truly believed it and was willing to throw my whole life away. I never saw any hope. I was alone and bewildered; I resorted to alcohol to numb the pain and anguish in my very soul. I slept off the disgust and woke up with a clear mind.

The hospital would have given me a hallucinate drug that would have the same affect, but would require hospitalization. I was able to get the affect from alcohol, thus avoiding hospital admittance. I was then able to have a fantastic Christmas with my wife's family and not worry them about my condition in hospital. Everything worked out perfectly with a few beers. I don't care what anyone says, alcohol does work in case of a crisis.

We all have a reason for living, and I think I found mine. I was put on this earth to help others just like me. Together, we can survive. Being alone, you are sure to die. That is why these services are available. If you are hungry, go to the soup kitchen. If you are tired, you can go to an emergency shelter for a night's sleep. There are several agencies designed with your interest in heart.

The newsletter informs the needy of what services are available and gives them contact information. There are people out there that can help you with a number of problems including housing, income assistance, and drug rehabilitation. Their waiting list may be long for these services for there is a high demand for them. Be patient.

In the meantime, you could build your support system of friends, family, councillors, doctors, or even the clergy. I give inspirational and moral support through my newsletter along with useful information. This compassion was born and inbred into me from my aunt and uncle. They constantly reminded me to treat others, as I would like to be treated. This is who I am.

I have compassion for my fellow man. I honestly care and pray for each one of them. I make an effort to be kind and understanding to them. There is too much hatred in this world, and I try to change that by starting with myself.

It is my hope that others will share my passion of goodwill and pass it on to their friends. Life is so much easier when accompanied by a smile. I had my share of sadness, and I know how hard it is to smile when you are down. I have to put extra effort to see through the dark clouds. My whole life was darkened by negativity; it is difficult to see that silver lining. Somehow, I have to put things aside and move on.

I think my doctor is correct that I have been shrouded by negativity all my life, and I have become accustomed to it. It's not that I like it; it is that I have gotten used to always feeling bad about myself. I don't see the good things in life anymore. It seems that this conclusion may be justified considering the facts.

That may be the reason for my delusion into the darkness. I could never see colour or light. Everything was in shades of black. I felt comfortable in the darkness. I have grown accustomed to it, and, in a way, I have enjoyed it. I found comfort and security deep in the folds of darkness. I would always retreat to my safe place in case of trouble.

This must be what the doctor meant about me accepting it as part of my life. I did cut myself off from reality where happiness and joy could not possibly enter. I protected myself too well. I barricaded myself into the darkness where nothing could touch me, not even love. Now, I understand. The signs were so visible that even my doctor noticed it. I just did not comprehend his terminology. I suppressed all emotions so that all I ever felt was numbness. I was content without having to deal with my emotions so my mind, heart, and soul shut down.

In a way, I did slip away from reality because I blocked it out. I remained hidden with my own thoughts in my own private world. The darkness was my home since I was a toddler growing up with an alcoholic father. Until now, I had blocked those memories from affecting me. That is why so much of my childhood memories are lost forever. I didn't want to remember them; they were too painful. This was true for most of my life spanning over four decades. I was hurting inside, and I couldn't handle it anymore. Reality was no longer a factor. I lived deep inside my own mind conjuring a world of security and safety from harm. After years of negativity, I found refuge by shutting out the world and there I would remain in the darkest corner of my mind.

I have grown accustomed to blocking out life in general with no desire to spread my wings and live again. That is where I died. My mind died, taking with it was my heart and soul. This is a major breakthrough in my life. I now realize what has happened to me. The two influential people of this discovery were my doctor and editor. Both of them knew that something happened early in my life that had a major impact on which I am today. They both knew that it was traumatic enough to change my thoughts on life. They gave me a time line to work from and I went on from there.

I honestly did not remember those thoughts that they said I had. It was so far back in my mind that what they were talking about was a mystery. I believed that my early childhood only consisted of good times. I was wrong. There were problems, but I couldn't handle them, so I blocked them out. I had to make the realization that my mentor had serious problems at one time during his life. The man that I loved as a father was not that perfect as I believed, and that hurt my thoughts and spirit about him.

However, he overcame his demons and his silver armour shone

through. He was my hero after all. It is time for me to take over where he left off and face my demons as well. If I want to be a man, I have to act like one too. The secret of my mind has been revealed. There are no more places to hide. I have to face life by confronting it at full speed.

I was so deep into my own mind that I truly believed that another world existed. It took two other people to make me realize that this was not true. I had to discover this on my own, on my own terms. Now, I see the light at the end of the tunnel. There is colour in my life once again. The darkness was a creation of my own mind. Perhaps at one time this was useful to prevent me from harm, but I no longer need that security. This place was only a figment of my imagination.

The sooner I realize this, the sooner I will be able to heal. I was in denial that this happened to me. My doctor saw through this and tried to make me understand. I wouldn't believe him or give him a chance.

Now, I understand and believe. This is a magnificent discovery. The secret of the darkness no longer exists. There are no places to hide anymore. I have to face the world head on. No longer numbed by the darkness, I can feel once again. This is not to say there will never be sadness in my life, but there will also be happiness and joy.

This delusion kept me away from living life as a normal human being. It felt so real that I believed it with all my heart. The darkness overwhelmed me--I believed and was trapped.

I really did block out reality. I was swimming within my own distorted thoughts. It took a lot of thinking to realize this. Distorted and confused, I went on with life hidden from the truths. The truth may have driven me over the edge at one time, but I am now mature enough to handle those truths like a man.

It is as if I just opened my eyes for the first time. Everything is brand new. This is the discovery that I have been looking for my entire life. I feared life, so I hid in the shadows of darkness. Today, I don't have to hide anymore. I am a man.

Love

I must learn from my wife the power of love. I can learn a great deal from this woman. You would not believe the torture that I have put her through over the past twenty-three years. She has been faithful and by my side through some pretty rough times, yet she never strayed.

The spouses have left all the people I know with this illness. I do not know anyone else that is still married. My wife is very special for she understands that it is an illness and that it is not my fault. She knows the effects of the illness and could distinguish it from the real me.

Kathy took her wedding vows very seriously, as did I. She must still see glimpses of the real me from time to time to keep her enthused.

When I first tried a suicide attempt, everyone was coaxing and asking her if she was going to leave me. Angrily she told them where to go and how to get there. Even the doctor and hospital questioned her about her next move. She stood by me when everyone else abandoned me. She fought tooth and nail, defending me from the ruthlessness of outsiders.

Even her best friend was trying to convince her to leave me. I am forever grateful to my wife because of the hell I put her through. She had all the valid reasons for leaving me, but somehow something deep inside of her told her to stay.

I've been ill for so long now that there are only short periods of good times. When healthy, I will make a spur of the moment decision to go for a walk with her and the dog. This catches her completely off guard for usually I do not do that. The illness zaps the energy from my body, leaving very little interest in other things. This is a big deal. It may seam minor, but even walking the dog can be too overwhelming for a person suffering mental illness. These little things remind my wife of the way I used to be. She loves going out for a family walk. Kathy enjoys the slightest effort towards my well-being.

She is very grateful for the most minor things I do for her. Even a simple dinner on the table pleases her till no end. I am very lucky to have her. If it were not for her support, it is most likely I would have been dead or in jail by now.

I used to come home at six o'clock in the morning all drunk and bloody. She would patch my wounds, give me my pills, and put me to bed before going to work. She never questioned why I was out all night. Even though my behaviour was questionable, she still trusted me. She accepted this behaviour as part of the illness and knew that I would be all right for the next several months until the next episode.

She also knew of my hyper libido and wandering eye. I used to flirt with other women right in front of her. Even this behaviour was tolerated. This is a remarkable woman. She had no idea what I was doing while I was out on an episode. It was just pure luck that nothing happened concerning other women. This was not from the lack of trying though.

I used to go out and have drinks with her. As we would leave, I would take off and hide while at the same time I was cutting myself. She would have to search the streets for me at all odd hours of the morning. I was totally out of control, yet she never turned me in or said a harsh word against me. Most people I know would never put up with that bullshit, but she has. I really don't know why she has stuck by my side after all those years of turmoil. Now she has to put up with my extravagant spending habits and alcoholism. At least we don't have to worry about the hyper libido anymore, for it has been controlled by medication. We also don't have to concern ourselves about psychosis for that has been treated as well.

The biggest problem we face together is my alcoholism. I know for a fact that this is extremely bothersome to my wife for she does not know how to deal with it.

She comes home at night and there isn't dinner on the table and the dog has not been taken care of. I am getting pissed at the neighbourhood bar. This is very hard on my wife for she knows that I have spent a lot of money on booze for a one-night piss up. She would rather I drink at home at a fraction of the cost.

The only reason I like going to the bar is for the interaction of my friends. It is a lonely life sitting at home for twenty-four hours a day. I still think my wife would rather have them come to the house to drink. Not is it only cheaper, she also has better control of the situation. She never said that I can't have friends, but she doesn't want me to go to the bar.

I could get pissed to the gills at home for fewer than forty dollars. At the bar, I could spend well over a hundred dollars to do the same thing and still not get drunk. My wife wants me at home and I can't blame her for wanting that.

With all this crap going on, she is still there for me no matter how much she hurts inside. I always wonder what is it that makes her stay. She has ample reasons to leave me, yet she doesn't. Could her love be that strong for me? I know that I worship the ground she walks on, but can she also feel the same way as I do?

It must be love. There is no other explanation why she would put up with such torture and take this kind of punishment. Her will to love is stronger than any other person I have ever met. She is committed to a long and happy life together as partners. That was my promise to her. She is a woman of her word, and nothing will come between us except death. Even then, I believe our connection is spiritual not physical. She is my soul mate.

I know her words without making a sound. I know her intentions without a gesture. I can see her love through her eyes. I feel her gentleness without touching. We are truly in love with each other.

This love deepens with every passing year. Not a minute goes by that I don't think of her. I automatically panic if she is five minutes late coming home from work. I pray to God that she will come home safe and sound. She is always on my mind. I love her very much.

My wife always takes care of my affairs such as bill payments, mediation, chores, and others. She is always there to back me up. This is a goldmine of wealth to have a treasure like her. I am truly blessed.

My dear aunt has loved me all her life. She brought me up with a compassionate heart, which I inherited from her. Her love was unconditional. There were times when I did not deserve it, but she was there anyway. She provided me with a happy and secure home. She soothed my fears and guided me into life as a gentle and loving man.

She made sure that I grew up with God in my heart. This inbred faith has been part of my life ever since. My aunt shunned sex and violence and provided a gentle environment. Even today, her love is unyielding. She is concerned and worried about my drinking. My aunt wants me to stop, but even her words have no meaning. My aunt knows all about alcoholism from my uncle, and she does not want me to be like he was when he was drinking.

With all this support and love, I still cannot break away from the alcohol. My wife's parents and siblings also love and support me. They are always there at a moment's notice. They have been by our side ever since I met their daughter. They have never strayed. I even have friends that are going to stop drinking in support of my own efforts. Everyone is on my side, and yet I cannot find the strength to stop drinking.

I am surrounded by love from my friends and family ready to support me in all my endeavours. Yet this does not seem to matter to me. I have abandoned them so that I could continue drinking. It seems for me that alcohol is more powerful than love. I have so much to be grateful for, and yet I don't appreciate what everyone is trying to do. This is shameful behaviour.

I have doctors and a counsellor trying to help me, yet I am in defiance. I have everything in place to become successful in quitting my addiction, yet something is holding me back. I have to acknowledge my friends, family, and supporters before they give up hope on me. I have to make the effort to be a man free from the chains that hold me down.

The way I am acting now seems that alcohol is more important than my wife. My priorities are all mixed up. I love my wife with all my heart, but I don't show it or act that way. I am ashamed of myself for being this way. It is demoralizing and hurtful. I am hurting all these people, maybe not intentionally, but indirectly.

My wife waits up at night waiting for her drunken husband to come home. This hurts her deeply, yet I do not see this. It seems that I don't have any thoughts of how I hurt people that I love. My self-esteem is at an all time low. The only thing that numbs the pain is alcohol. My personal needs seem to be more important than anyone else, and this is wrong.

I have all these valid reasons to change my ways, yet I neglect them and push them aside. I cannot see that people care for me very deeply. They want the best for me and I turn a blind eye. Why can't I see what they are trying to do for me? The booze is controlling my life and ruining me. Why can't I see this?

I am hurting people; especially the one I love the most. My wife had nothing but turmoil living with me, and yet she still puts up with me. She is a truly remarkable woman. Even if I did stop drinking, I could never make up for what I have done to her. However, that would be a start in the right direction.

The right thing to do is to go through detox again and try the residential rehabilitation program. I have to find the strength somewhere to take that plunge. I owe at least this much to my friends and family.

I joined a writer's group to see if I could improve my skills. I wanted to see what other writers were doing and maybe pick up a few pointers. It is a tight knit group who have all become close friends.

I have friends at the writer's group that also care for my plight and me. Prayers are being said on my behalf for my success in beating my demons. Everyone is on my side. Now, I have to do my part and fight back.

I never realized how lucky I really am. The support and love is in place, all I have to do is utilize it. Why am I so hesitant in helping myself towards a better life? I did it before and was a much better man for it until I got sick again. Maybe, I'm afraid of failure. I don't want to try again for the reason if I fail I will feel ashamed and belittled.

I have to realize that addiction is ongoing and there will be relapses. I just have to get back on the horse and try again. Last time I relapsed, I gave up hope and thought of myself as a failure. I threw in the towel and thought that it was useless to try again for I would only fail.

I don't know if I have the strength to pull me out of another relapse. My self-esteem was beaten, and I was down. I don't know if I can withstand any more failures. I presume that I am scared. That is why I am so resistant to help. I gave it my best shot, and I failed. That was very hurtful for I did my best to try to beat my demons.

The emotions involved with failure are overwhelming. The only thing I do to rid myself of that pain is to drink and go into my dark place. It is there that I find refuge from my emotions. I can numb them so that they do not hurt me. There I sit emotionless to the outside world.

Being so vulnerable to the outside due to my childhood, I can hide in my corner and wait for the emotions to pass. Being mild and gentle, I cannot handle the outside stresses of your world. The alcohol gives me courage and strength for yet another day.

Instead of hiding under the wing of my aunt, I use alcohol as my security blanket. I am unable to face your world. The darkness is my safe place away from harm. I have been hurt too much in my life to face yet another tragedy. So I numb myself to such a point that I can withstand the harsh realities.

Maybe, it was inevitable that I would become an alcoholic. The pieces to the puzzle are there. There was the up bringing, tragedy, environment, and illness. It has been my loved ones who kept me alive and out of jail.

It was the security of the darkness that kept me sane; otherwise, I would have been institutionalized. Without the darkness to protect me, I would have lost my sanity years ago.

Can I preserve my sanity if I quit drinking now? For a short time I may be able to stop until my next round of illness. Being desperate again, I would only seek refuge from the bottle. Then, it would start all over again. I don't want to fail anymore, but it seems inevitable that I will.

The illness has to be controlled for me to be successful. I cannot withstand the power of illness on my own. It might require that I be put in hospital for a short time to prevent relapse, but if that will work, it would be worth it.

If not, I will be backed into the corner with no recourse but to step into the darkness once again. Proper treatment is necessary to my survival. I need the medical system to back me up; I can't do it alone. I already tried that and failed.

Other than that, I have no other choice than to choose my dark place for refuge. My sanity is at stake. If it means rotting out my liver, so be it. Every day that I am alive is a blessing. I could only live one day at a time. If I have to erase those memories of those days, I will. This is done with the aid of alcohol and the darkness. Weeks, months, and years will quickly slip by me until God takes me to a better place.

My sanity is very important to me, and I will do everything in my power to keep it at whatever the cost. Losing control of my actions is the scariest thing I have ever had to face. At least drinking to a stupor will lessen the chances of losing control of my mind. In a way, I still lose control, but I am peaceful. I just hop in a cab, go home, and pass out till morning.

When I lose control of my mind that is when trouble starts. Sometimes, not even the booze will stop it if I don't catch it in time. Timing is very important. Alcohol is used as a preventive measure, not a cure, it can't help me while I am already in the grips of illness, and booze just fuels it. If I am in psychosis, the alcohol will magnify the effect of the illness turning me into a dangerous and unpredictable man.

Fortunately, I have medication to prevent that from happening. Now, all I have to deal with is the emotional and bipolar affects of illness. This is easier to control. Alcohol does numb these effects. It is a depressant itself and, in fact, it makes things worse, but you don't feel it. You are safe and content away from harm.

It is the security that I am addicted to. I am not strong enough to face the world on my own. Although the effects are only temporary, this does give me enough time to take a breather until the next day. Then I do it all over again. Thus, addiction is born.

This could have been inbred into my early years due to my insecurities. Without a male presence in my life, I was not shown what it takes to be a man. I was hidden from reality at an early age. When trouble started, I learned to develop this security on my own by blocking things out. I was hidden from the harshness that exists in life. I was nurtured and protected by my loving aunt, never to see the realities of the world.

When I saw something that invaded that security, I would block that out from memory. This started from the very beginning, living with an alcoholic uncle. I blocked all those memories from years gone by. I did not make that discovery until just recently. I found those memories threatening, and I blocked them out.

The arguments, staggering, and obnoxious behaviour were out of the norm. This was damaging to my soul. Drinking was all around me; there was no place to hide except deep inside. That is where the seed was planted. It was extremely unpleasant to see my mentor act this way. I looked up to him, and he wasn't there. This was too much to handle, so I suppressed those feelings for over forty years. I buried those thoughts deep within my soul. Now, those feelings are finding a way to vent out.

I numb those feelings with alcohol and stay behind the protection of the darkness where those feelings cannot penetrate me. This was the mystery that has been haunting me for all these years. My editor and doctor were correct that something happened to me very early in my life that has changed me forever.

I have to admit to myself that my mentor had weaknesses as well. He wasn't perfect like I believed. This is a remarkable discovery that may help towards my recovery. People were telling me that something happened early in my childhood, but I could not recall those memories. I was dumbfounded. I didn't know what they were talking about until now.

It is all making sense to me now. I found the hidden key to my life. This has unlocked the mystery that has had me bound for all these years. The one thing about my uncle is that he is still my hero, perhaps, more now than ever before, because he took control of his life and quit drinking.

Not only that, he also quit smoking for more than thirty years. Both addictions were beaten on his first attempt. He never looked back. My Uncle Adam was and still is my hero. I love him dearly.

Perhaps now I can move on. You have to fix the past before moving on with the future. I have done that now. This has been very enlightening indeed. Something buried so long ago that my memory was not able to pick it up. It took the persistence of my editor to make this discovery. He gave me a time frame to work from, and I did the soul searching.

Together we revealed the secrets to my past. This has been an awakening. All those negative memories are surfacing to the top. Perhaps now, the old wounds will heal. The doors are wide open and a new adventure begins. There is a sigh of relief knowing this. I was hiding all my life, burying the secrets with me. This is truly a time to celebrate.

I have no ill will towards my dearly departed uncle; in fact I am grateful for the good times we did have together. However, I am delighted that this burden has been lifted off from my shoulders. Revealing these secrets has changed my character for I feel whole again. For all those years, there was something missing. I feel complete again. This has been a tremendous journey and there really was a light at the end of the tunnel.

That was the last piece of the puzzle; now I have the picture. As unpleasant as it was to discover those sad feelings, it was terribly important to my well-being. Now, I can let go and move on. I feel good about myself once again. It is a re-birth to a whole new world full of discoveries yet to be seen. Today is a good day to be alive.

Those early formative years had a severe impact on what I am today. It cultured me into a mild-mannered and loving man. Non-aggressiveness and passivity are my major characteristics. I am thankful for that for it was this reason that has kept me out of jail during some very tempting times. My strong morals prevailed over the temptation of illness allowing me to sleep at night with a clear conscience. If I was more aggressive in my nature, I would not be able to withstand the power of temptation.

The thing that I cannot withstand now is my illness and alcoholism. I feel emotionally healed and that is great news. This has been a major obstacle in my life.

I now have gone full circle and understanding every detail of what happened in my life. I understand where I came from and how my problems developed. I now have closure in my life. I no longer have to live in the past or hide from it.

My life is an open book. This is how it all came about. Considering all the circumstances, I have done quite well for myself. Some of those blows were near fatal, ending my grasp on sanity and my life. Somehow, I survived. The nurturing of my aunt and uncle let me see the good things in life. However, when faced with negativity, I would hide deep inside my very soul. I was always afraid of life. That is why I blocked my emotions and hid in the confines of the darkness. It is there where I was locked up for over forty years of my life.

It is time now to embrace my loved ones and accept their love and support. I believe I have now found my strength within these pages. I have found God and myself.

This is very exciting for I see the world in a whole different light. I'm not afraid anymore. I embrace life with open arms. I no longer belong in the world of darkness. Those days are over. The pasture is much greener on this side of reality. It served its purpose when it was necessary, but now it is time to break free.

I can now rejoin the living and carry on into new dreams and adventures. There still will be challenges, but that is life, and I am ready for it. I have this inner peace in my heart that soothes my soul. The secrets are out, and I can live again free from torment and pain. I can go to bed tonight knowing that I am well taken care of.

I want to thank-you for allowing me to share my secrets with you. It has been a tremendous journey. This awakening is a start of a whole new life. God bless you.

Patrick J. Schnerch

About the Author

Something terrible happened to that little boy. At an early age, something damaged his heart and soul, sending him into the folds of darkness. There, Patrick Schnerch would hide from the emotional turmoil, which jeopardized his sanity. This delusional place was his sanctuary away from reality.

Trauma, up bringing, illness, and eventually alcoholism claimed yet another damaged soul. Decades would pass being oblivious to the real world. Trapped within the darkness, he would seek refuge from anything that could harm him.

Memories were blocked out from his past since he did not participate to the realities of your world. Only fragments of his tragic past could be recollected. The author was haunted by uncovered secrets, which were the basis of his demise. Suicidal and with no place to turn, he was at the crossroads of disaster.

Not quite being ready to cash in all his chips yet, Patrick had one more plan to execute to set him free. Dumbfounded at where to start looking for answers, he decided to unearth the details of his life starting at the very beginning and dissect every known memory in order to piece together an overall picture of his past.

He started documenting those painful memories in order to discover the cause of his turmoil on earth. Slowly, pieces were falling together creating a picture that was making sense, discoveries unknown to the author were being made clear.

Finally, after much soul searching, he found the missing key. He relived his horrors and found what he was looking for. He found his inner peace and was able to accept his past and put those torturous years behind him.

He now stands tall; free from the darkness that has engulfed him for the past forty years. There is hope and a future waiting him in this world of reality. There are now goals and ambitions for a new life; the author has now made peace with himself and God. It is time to move on.

About the Book

The book is a journey from early childhood to the far reaches of disassociation and insanity compounded with alcoholism. It describes the spawning of a very disturbed individual and discovers the onset of the damaging characteristics, which has followed the author till this present day.

This publication unveils the deepest and darkest secrets in order to accept and put to rest a traumatic life engulfed by negativity. It details every aspect, which caused irreparable damage to an otherwise, mild and loving demeanour.

The book goes into great detail of what life is like with mental illness and addiction. Dual Diagnosis is the given names for such conditions. In this case, alcohol was used to numb the affects of the illness. The illness became unbearable to cope with. Medications and therapy do not have the desired affects to calm a crisis, where alcohol is fast acting and gives almost instant temporary relief. This is why it is so addicting. The author was desperate to relieve himself from his painful and torturous life.

Unable to face reality, the author hid in the delusional world of disassociation blocking out your realm. He would hide in this secret world for decades away from the pains of reality. Secluded and alone, he would slip further into the abyss. The alcohol was used to induce this imaginary sanctuary into a new reality. Oblivious to reality, the author entered a place free from rules, regulations and morals. The most despicable swirling thoughts were compounding which was in fact changing his behaviour and character.

Normally a mild and loving demeanour, the author's character would develop into situations, which caused a threat to him and the public. The author slipped into a psychosis and his world turned to black. His character turned evil and demented with no hope of escape. Desperate of staying in control, he used self-mutilation and alcohol to calm the beast. Bloody and intoxicated, he would wander the streets in the early morning hours searching for answers.

ISBN 141209508-5